MAKING

AND USING

SCIENTIFIC

EQUIPMENT

MAKING
AND USING
SCIENTIFIC
EQUIPMENT
DAVID E. NEWTON

AN EXPERIMENTAL
SCIENCE BOOK

FRANKLIN WATTS
NEW YORK/CHICAGO/TORONTO
LONDON/SYDNEY

Diagrams by Vantage Art

Photographs copyright ©: The Bettmann Archive: pp. 14 top, 15; Photo Researchers, Inc.: pp. 14 bottom, 18 (David Parker/SPL), 63 (Hal H. Harrison/NAS), 88 bottom (Guy Gillette), 120 (Jon Brenneis); Historical Pictures/Stock Montage, Inc.: pp. 17, 48 top; Burndy Library: p. 32 top; Taylor Products: p. 32 bottom; Brown Brothers, Sterling, PA: pp. 40, 62; Shimadzu Scientific Instruments, Inc.: p. 48 bottom; Utrechts Universiteitsmuseum Trans: p. 87 top; Bausch & Lomb: p. 87 bottom; Nikon, Melville, NY: p. 88 top; Salvatore Tocci: pp. 141, 143, 144, 146.

Library of Congress Cataloging-in-Publication Data

Newton, David E.
    Making and using scientific equipment / David E. Newton.
    p.   cm.—(An Experimental science book)
    Includes bibliographical references and index.
    Summary: Describes the function of scientific equipment used in the fields of physics, meteorology, biology, and earth science and provides instructions for constructing these instruments.
    ISBN 0-531-11176-8—ISBN 0-531-15663-X
    1. Scientific apparatus and instruments—Design and construction. 2. Scientific apparatus and instruments. [1. Scientific apparatus and instruments.] I. Title. II. Series.
    Q185.N55 1993
    681'.75—dc20   92-38039 CIP AC

CONTENTS

To Richard Olson and John McArdle,
with many thanks for many kind deeds
and many good times

MAKING

AND USING

SCIENTIFIC

EQUIPMENT

1

MAKING AND
USING SCIENTIFIC
EQUIPMENT

Start with a piece of wood, a soda straw, some string and cardboard and a fishing weight. Add a little imagination and some hard work and you will have a clinometer, a device for measuring the slope of a hill or valley.

We read and hear a lot today about sophisticated scientific instruments such as electron microscopes, radio telescopes, and particle accelerators. Scientists use these instruments to discover new information about the nature of matter and the universe. But the amateur scientist can learn a great deal about the natural world with simple devices that can be built at little cost and with modest effort.

WHY BUILD YOUR OWN SCIENTIFIC EQUIPMENT?

You might ask why you should bother to build your own equipment. Most people can buy or bor-

[11]

row devices like those described in this book. That is certainly easier than doing the work yourself.

Most people who do build their own scientific equipment do so for one of two reasons or both. First, some people just like doing the work themselves. Making your own solar heater or balance or microscope is an interesting challenge. You can feel a sense of accomplishment at starting with simple raw materials and ending up with a tool that actually works. Like an artist, this kind of person builds equipment not just to have it but to have worked on it.

Second, some people build equipment in order to use it in experiments, activities, and projects. Someone who wants to study water pollution, for example, may want to build his or her own Secchi disk rather than buy one at a scientific supply company. A Secchi disk is fairly easy to build, and it can be used to determine the murkiness of a pond or lake.

Sometimes a person may have to build a piece of equipment. He or she may want to do an experiment that has never been done before, and the right piece of equipment may not even exist. You will probably not build an entirely new piece of equipment. But you may well decide to modify a piece of equipment described in this book.

Throughout history, scientists have built much of the equipment they needed in order to do original research. In many cases, the equipment they needed just didn't exist. For example, in the seventeenth century, when Galileo decided to study motion, he couldn't go to the nearest supply store and buy what he needed. He had to construct an inclined plane and other equipment he wanted for his research. Robert Gardner's book on *Famous*

Experiments You Can Do listed in the Bibliography, describes more such inventions.

One instrument that has experienced tremendous development over the years is the telescope. Photo 1 shows Galileo's telescope; Photo 2, the 200-inch telescope at Mt. Palomar; and Photo 3, the Hubble space telescope.

Much of the equipment familiar to chemists today was invented by alchemists in the Middle Ages. Flasks, retorts, burners, furnaces, stills, and mortar and pestles were all invented in the fruitless search to find ways to turn lead into gold.

In many cases, pieces of equipment still carry the names of scientists who first designed them: the Bunsen burner, Erlenmeyer flask, Petri dish, Welsbach gas mantle, Wheatstone bridge, and Newtonian reflecting telescope are only a few examples. Even more common is the tendency of scientists to modify existing equipment to make it more effective or to use it in a new way. As just one example, in 1912 the English physicist J. J. Thomson used a simple glass tube connected to a battery to study the atomic weight of neon. He was confused by the results he obtained and assigned the problem to one of his students, Francis Aston. Aston took the idea of the glass tube and modified it to produce a new instrument, a mass spectrograph. Aston used the mass spectrograph not only to solve the problem of neon's atomic weight but also to determine the atomic weights of nearly every other element.

One of the best examples of improving on someone's else's scientific equipment is found in the field of particle accelerators. The first accelerator was built by Ernest O. Lawrence at the University of California at Berkeley in the early 1930s. Lawrence used coffee cans, sealing wax, and left-

Photos 1 and 2. The first telescope (inset), built
by Galileo in the early seventeenth century.
The 200-inch Hale telescope at Mt. Palomar,
for many years the largest telescope in the world.

PHOTO 3. The Hubble space telescope,
the most powerful telescope ever built

over laboratory equipment to make his 4.3-inch cyclotron. A year later he built a second machine that was bigger (9.8 inches in diameter) and better than the first. Photo 4 shows an early cyclotron.

Over the past six decades, physicists have continued to improve on Lawrence's original idea, making accelerators that are larger, more powerful, and more sophisticated. Today, construction goes on near Waxahachie, Texas, on the latest version of the particle accelerator, the superconducting super collider (SSC). When completed, the SSC will be about 52 miles in circumference, a million times larger than Lawrence's original machine.

One section of another modern particle accelerator is shown in Photo 5. This device is nearly 17 miles in diameter and is thousands of times more powerful than Lawrence's early cyclotrons.

The historical lesson, then, is that equipment can always be modified and improved. Keep that in mind as you read through the descriptions of the instruments and other equipment in this book. Think about ways in which a piece of equipment can be made better or changed for some other use that you can think of.

USING SCIENTIFIC EQUIPMENT FOR PROJECTS

Some of the equipment described in this book is primarily "helper" equipment. Devices such as thermometers and balances are used in a great variety of experiments and activities, some of which are presented in this book. Using this equipment can be an interesting way to learn some basic ideas about science.

PHOTO 4. The American scientist Ernest O. Lawrence
(right), his student M. Stanley Livingston, and one of
their early atom smashers at the University of
California at Berkeley

Photo 5. One of the atom smashers at CERN, the European Center for Particle Physics in Geneva, Switzerland

Other equipment can be put to use immediately in research. Once built, the rain gauge, spectroscope, and calorimeter, for example, will be useful in answering questions about the natural world. The "Additional Projects" listed at the end of each section describe additional investigations that can be attacked with each piece of equipment. In this book there are approximately 130 activities and projects using the equipment you build. But you will probably be able to think of even more ways to use your homemade apparatuses.

These projects are often fun and interesting to do alone or with a friend. Or they may be used to satisfy a class assignment or as a science fair project. If you are thinking of a science fair project, talk to your adult partner or a science teacher first to make sure that what you do qualifies for a science fair. Then, if you are interested in going for a prize, make sure that it will stand you a chance to win.

More ambitious readers may want to combine scientific equipment into a larger project. For example, you could measure the effect of temperature on transpiration by using both the thermometer and the potometer described in this book. Or, you could build your own weather station using the thermometer, barometer, anemometer, and hair hygrometer.

Another possibility is to work with friends on a group of related projects. For example, each person in the group might build an instrument for a "historical laboratory" (astrolabe, water clock, air thermometer, etc.), for a weather station (described above), or a pollution-testing lab (thermometer, Secchi disk, distilling apparatus, etc.).

CALIBRATING INSTRUMENTS

Many of the instruments described in this book must be calibrated before they can be used. The word *calibration* means "to establish a scale." You set the scale by comparing the instrument being calibrated with some standard instrument. For example, the water clock will keep track of time by allowing drops of water to escape from a bottle at a regular rate. To calibrate the water clock, you need to compare that rate against some known standard device for measuring time, such as a clock or watch.

SUPPLIES

You should have little problem finding sources for the materials needed to build the equipment in this book. Items like cardboard boxes, pieces of wood, glass jars, rubber bands, and pieces of paper are readily available around the house or at local lumber yards, hardware stores, or office supply stores.

Your science teacher will be the best source for specialized equipment such as screw clamps, rubber stoppers, and glass tubing. Any item that he or she cannot supply should be available from a scientific supply house. Ask your teacher for further information, or refer to Appendix 2 for further suggestions.

SAFETY

Most of the tools and materials mentioned in this book are safe to use. You should be certain that you know how to use a saw and other simple tools, however. It is a good idea to find an adult partner to answer questions about materials and techniques with which you are not familiar, help you find materials, and work with you. The adult partner should ideally be a science teacher or professional scientist, but could also be another adult *knowledgeable about scientific procedures and the safety considerations involved.*

In the instructions for building equipment and in the projects and activities that follow, references are often made to this adult partner and sometimes to a qualified science teacher, scientist, or other professional. Even though such references are not made on each page, supervision is essential during all stages of both making and using scientific equipment—planning the work; conducting the work; displaying the work; cleaning up, dismantling, or storing the work.

In those few directions for building and using equipment when potentially dangerous materials or methods are used, you will find a *Safety Note* or *Caution* telling you when risks may be involved in making or using a piece of equipment. Read these warnings carefully and pay attention to them as you work.

You should also get in the habit of remembering some general safety rules in doing any kind of science project. The following list includes some of those rules. Talk with your adult partner about these rules and any other rules she or he may recommend to you.

1.   Always work under supervision of your adult partner. Never conduct any project without the advice and approval of that partner. Never do any field study or experiment without your adult partner present.

2.   Always wear approved safety goggles when building your equipment or doing a project with it. Working with chemicals or power tools is the obvious time to wear goggles, but you should wear them at all other times too, however harmless the activity seems.

3.   Always wear a lab apron, lab coat, or some other kind of protective clothing when working in a lab or with hazardous materials anywhere.

4.   Always assume that any chemical is toxic (poisonous) and harmful to your eyes, nose, skin, and clothing. Many chemicals are *not* dangerous. But you will be safer if you treat all chemicals with great respect.

5.   Be very cautious with open flames.

6.   Use special care when heating any object. Normally you will use a Bunsen or alcohol burner to heat containers. Have your adult partner demonstrate the correct method for using these burners.

7.   Always know where safety equipment is located and how to use it. The safety equipment you should know about includes a fire extinguisher, an eyewash, a safety shower, and a fire blanket.

8.   Always keep your work area neat and clean. A messy work space can cause serious accidents.

WORKING WITH GLASS

Many projects in the book require that you work with glass. Improper handling of glass can be dangerous. Most people have less experience cutting and bending glass than they do sawing boards and hammering nails. For this reason, a special section on glass work is provided in Appendix 1 at the back of this book. Read through Appendix 1 before working on any project that involves the use of glass. You may also find that learning more about working with glass is an interesting project in and of itself.

KEEPING RECORDS

An important part of any science project is keeping good records. You may want to look back at some time in the future to see what you did while building or using scientific equipment. Buy a notebook in which you can record your work. Your science teacher may have suggestions about the kinds of records to keep. Normally you should write down the purpose for which you built the equipment, the kinds of materials you used, the steps you took in building and using the equipment, the observations you made with it, and any conclusions you drew as a result of your work. You may also want to make diagrams of the work you did.

GOING FURTHER

Much of the equipment described in this book is simple to make. You should be able to build it and have it ready to use in a short time. When you have finished a piece of equipment, think of all the ways you can use it in your home, in your neighborhood, or at school. You may be surprised at some of the new projects that may occur to you.

For example, you can find out the temperature today by listening to the radio or television, by reading the newspaper, or by looking at the thermometer outside the kitchen window. But how does the temperature vary at different locations in your home? None of these sources can answer that question for you, but your homemade thermometer will.

Maybe the answer you get will suggest further research. For example, what does it mean if you find out that one room of the house is always warmer or colder than another room? Perhaps you can make changes in the way your house is heated that will help you conserve energy. If you do move beyond the scope of this book, be sure to do so only after consultation with your adult partner.

It is not difficult to see how even the simplest instrument can lead to projects that can be used in a science fair or a science class. However, not all projects have to be fancy or complicated. One appealing result of building scientific equipment is simply to find out interesting things about the world around you.

2

EQUIPMENT FOR MAKING MEASUREMENTS

What's happening in the world around you? Maybe that seems like a simpleminded question. But it's easy to take the everyday events of life for granted, to miss out on changes to which most people pay little attention.

For example, how long each day does the sun shine through your bedroom (or living room or kitchen) window? If there are plants in the room, you might want to know the answer to this question. Most plants require some minimum amount of sunlight in order to grow and stay healthy.

Both scientists and nonscientists may find questions like this one interesting. The equipment—measuring instruments—described in this chapter provide the simplest and most basic answers to such questions as: how long did it take? (water clock), how warm is it? (thermometers), and how much does it weigh? (spring balance).

See the Bibliography for books containing additional projects using these instruments.

WATER CLOCK

Any timing device operates on the principle of periodic motion, that is, a movement of some kind that is repeated at regular intervals. For example, time is measured in a grandfather clock by the regular back and forth motion of a pendulum. Early humans used simple periodic motions as a way of keeping time: the drip of water out of a container, the flow of sand from one glass bulb to another, or the regular heartbeat that can be detected in a person's pulse.

The water clock described below is an example of a primitive but accurate method of keeping time. It can be used in a variety of projects in which accurate time measurements are not essential. You can measure periods of a few minutes quite easily, but not periods of time much less than that. For example, in an experiment on animal behavior, you might want to know how much food a gerbil eats in 15 minutes at various times of the day.

Safety Note. Review the cautions in Appendix 1 about working with glass. Work under supervision and wear safety goggles and a lab coat or lab apron. Use caution in working with flames.

Materials: triangular file; pencil and ruler; glass tubing, at least 4 inches long; Bunsen or alcohol burner; 1-hole rubber stopper; rubber tubing, at least 3 inches long; screw clamp; scissors; 1-quart or 1-liter plastic bottle; cardboard box a least 2 feet deep, with one side off; glue; strip of white paper, as long as the tall jar and about 2 inches wide; tall glass or plastic jar with straight sides, whose volume must be greater than that of the bottle; hammer and nail; watch or clock.

Directions

Note: Letters in parentheses—for example, (A)—are keyed in to Figure 1.

1. Read the instructions in Appendix 1 about cutting and fire-polishing glass tubing. Then, cut and fire-polish a piece of the glass tubing about 4 inches long.

2. Read the instructions in Appendix 1 about inserting glass tubing into a rubber stopper. Then, carefully insert the glass tubing (A) into the rubber stopper (B) so that about ¼ inch of tubing extends beyond the small end of the stopper.

3. Attach about 3 inches of the rubber tubing (C) to the long end of the glass tubing. Tighten the screw clamp (D) on the rubber tubing.

4. With the scissors, carefully make a hole the same diameter as the quart (or liter) bottle (E) in the bottom of the cardboard box (F). The bottle will have to fit tightly into this hole.

5. Glue the strip of white paper (G) to one side of the tall jar (H). The time scale will later be written on this paper.

6. Fill the quart (or liter) bottle with water and insert the rubber stopper tightly. Make sure the screw clamp is closed.

7. Tip the bottle upside down and place it in the hole in the cardboard box. With the hammer and nail, make a small hole (I) in the bottom of the quart (or liter) bottle. Place the tall jar beneath the

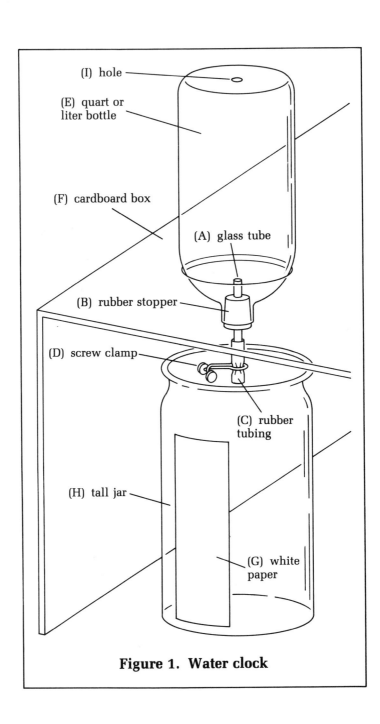

(I) hole

(E) quart or liter bottle

(F) cardboard box

(A) glass tube

(B) rubber stopper

(D) screw clamp

(C) rubber tubing

(H) tall jar

(G) white paper

Figure 1. Water clock

quart (or liter) bottle so that the end of the rubber tube fits inside the neck of the tall jar.

Calibrating the Clock

Loosen the screw clamp so that water comes out of the rubber tubing one drop at a time. Use the watch or clock to note how much water drips into the tall jar in 5 minutes. Draw a line on the white paper that corresponds to the water level after 5 minutes. Repeat this process at 5-minute intervals until the quart (or liter) bottle is empty. You may wish to change the scale on the tall jar by increasing or decreasing the flow of water from the quart (or liter) bottle.

Projects

1.   Select a series of normal daily events to time. You might include a half-hour television program, the length of a school class, or the time for a 3-minute egg timer to empty. Choose events that range in length from short to long. Decide the time periods over which your water clock seems to be most accurate.

2.   Use your experience in making the water clock to make a sand clock. Calibrate the sand clock using the water clock.

3.   Compare the accuracies of the water and sand clocks. Find out in which situations each is more accurate or more convenient.

4.   Some scientific experiments can be timed using your water clock. For example, use your clock to find out how long an ice cube takes to melt in a glass of water. Then, see how the melting time changes when you vary the temperature of the water in the glass. How does the melting time vary if

[29]

you use different volumes of water at the same temperature? Find out how the speed of melting depends on the size of an ice cube.

THERMOMETERS

Until the sixteenth century, humans had no instruments for measuring temperatures. Of course, they could say that something was "hot" or "warm" or "cold." But there was no instrument to say that the temperature was 20°C or 70°F. Then, in 1593, Galileo invented the first thermometer. His "thermoscope" was a simple device, much like the gas thermometer described below. As air trapped inside a glass tube was warmed or cooled, it expanded or contracted, causing a liquid to move downward or upward in the tube. This liquid movement provided a way of expressing temperature in a quantitative, or numerical way. When Galileo's contemporary Sanctorius adapted the thermoscope to fit into a person's mouth, the first clinical thermometer was created.

Gas thermometers have a number of disadvantages, and most common thermometers today are liquid thermometers. Temperature changes are measured by the expansion or contraction of a liquid in a narrow glass tube. The earliest liquid thermometers used water or alcohol as the liquid. In 1714, however, the German-Dutch physicist Gabriel Fahrenheit showed how liquid thermometers using mercury could be more effective than those using water or alcohol. Today, mercury thermometers are the most common of all accurate thermometers.

The thermometers you make for this project can be used to measure temperatures where a high degree of accuracy is not necessary. For example, you can use them to compare the temperatures two days in a row, which can be helpful in making weather predictions.

Photo 6 shows thermometers used in an experiment conducted about 200 years ago. Photo 7 shows a modern digital thermometer.

GAS (AIR) THERMOMETER

Safety Note: Review the cautions in Appendix 1 about working with glass. Work under supervision and wear safety goggles and a lab coat or lab apron while working on this project. Use caution in working with flames.

Materials: hammer; nails; glue; piece of wood, 1 inch × 8 inches × 8 inches; piece of wood, 2 inches × 8 inches × 12 inches; triangular file; pencil and ruler; glass tubing, at least 9 inches long; Bunsen or alcohol burner; 1-hole rubber stopper to fit one bottle; two glass or plastic bottles, each about 1 pint in volume; candle wax; two thin aluminum or copper strips, 1 inch × 8 inches; tacks; water colored with food coloring; light machine oil; white cardboard, about 1 inch × 4 inches; hair dryer; commercial thermometer.

Directions

Note: Letters in parentheses—for example, (A)— are keyed in to Figure 2.

1. Make a support stand by nailing or gluing the 1 inch × 8 inch × 8 inch board (A) to the 2 inch × 8 inch × 12 inch board (B).

2. Read the instructions in Appendix 1 about cutting and fire-polishing glass tubing. Then, cut

PHOTO 6. Early thermometers

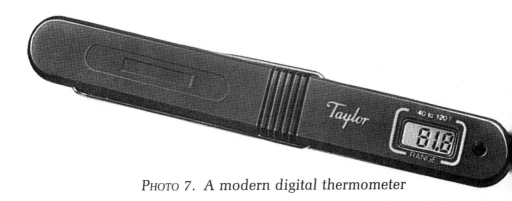

PHOTO 7. A modern digital thermometer

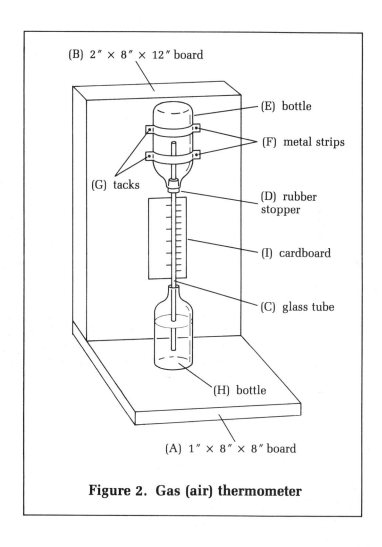

Figure 2. Gas (air) thermometer

and fire-polish a piece of glass tubing about 9 inches long.

3.   Read the instructions in Appendix 1 about inserting glass tubing into a stopper. Then, carefully insert the glass tube (C) into the rubber stopper (D).

[33]

4. Insert the rubber stopper into one of the bottles (E). With the candle wax or glue, seal the stopper to the bottle and the glass tube to the stopper.

5. Attach the bottle upside down to the support stand. Bend the metal strips (F) around the bottle, pull them very tightly against the stand, and attach them with tacks (G).

6. Fill the second bottle (H) with the colored water. Place it on the base of the stand so that the glass tube extends into the lower bottle. Place one drop of the light machine oil on top of the colored water to reduce evaporation of the liquid.

7. Attach the white cardboard (I) to the vertical piece of wood.

Calibrating the Air Thermometer
Heat the upper bottle with the hair dryer. The air in the bottle will expand, and bubbles will escape through the glass tube into the lower bottle. Turn off the dryer after about ten bubbles have escaped. Allow the homemade thermometer to sit for about 10 minutes. Then place it in a warm location where the temperature is known. Note the level to which the liquid in the glass tube drops. Read the temperature in this location on the commercial thermometer. Mark the level of the colored liquid on the cardboard. Write down the temperature that corresponds to this level.

Place the homemade thermometer in a cool location where the temperature is known. Repeat the above process to find the highest level to which the water rises in the glass tube.

Finally, divide the distance between the upper and lower lines on the card into ten equal spaces. Determine and write down the temperatures that correspond to each space.

LIQUID (WATER) THERMOMETER

Safety Note: Review the cautions in Appendix 1 about working with glass. Work under supervision and wear safety goggles and a lab coat or lab apron while working on this project. Use caution in working with flames. Use pot holders when handling the pan of boiling water.

Materials: glass or plastic bottle with capacity of about 1 quart (or 1 liter); water colored with food coloring dye; glass tubing, at least 24 inches long; Bunsen or alcohol burner; one-hole rubber stopper to fit bottle; trivet; pan of boiling water; glass-marking pencil or adhesive tape; bucket of cold water; ice; commercial thermometer; white paper; scissors; pencil or pen; ruler; cellophane tape; watch or clock that registers seconds.

Directions

Note: Letters in parentheses—for example, (A)—are keyed in to Figure 3.

1. Fill the bottle (A) with colored water (B) to the top.

2. Read the instructions in Appendix 1 about cutting and fire-polishing glass tubing. Then, cut and fire-polish a piece of glass tubing about 24 inches long.

3. Read the instructions in Appendix 1 about inserting glass tubing into a stopper. Then, insert the glass tube (C) into the rubber stopper (D).

[35]

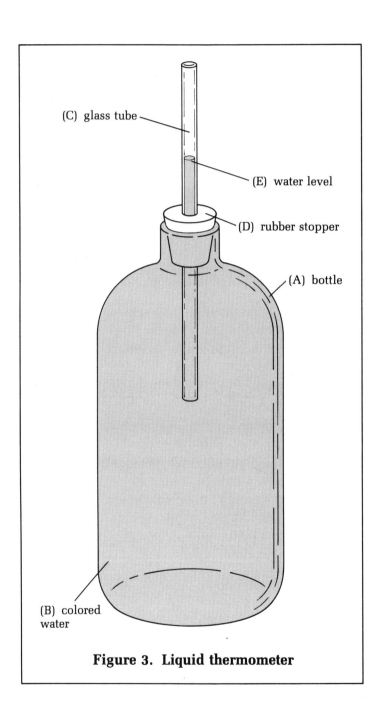

(C) glass tube

(E) water level

(D) rubber stopper

(A) bottle

(B) colored water

Figure 3. Liquid thermometer

4. Carefully insert the rubber stopper into the bottle. Some of the colored water in the bottle will be forced out as you do this. Make sure that no air is trapped inside the bottle. Push the stopper in tightly so that the colored water rises a small distance (E) into the glass tube.

Calibrating the Water Thermometer

Bring a large pan of water to a boil. Use pot holders to remove the boiling water from the heat. Set the pan of boiling water on a fireproof area or place it on a trivet. Slowly place the water thermometer into the pan of boiling water. When the colored water in the tube stops rising for about 15 seconds, mark the highest level it reaches with the glass-marking pencil or a piece of the adhesive tape. Read the temperature of the hot water with the commercial thermometer. Record this temperature as the boiling point of water.

Remove the water thermometer from the boiling water, allow it to cool to room temperature, and place it in the bucket of cold water. Add ice to the water slowly while stirring. Observe the temperature of the water with the commercial thermometer. When the colored water reaches the top of the bottle, note the temperature on the commercial thermometer. Record this temperature as the lowest temperature your thermometer can read.

With the scissors, cut a piece of the white paper long enough to reach from the top of the bottle to the highest mark. Mark the temperatures on the top and bottom of the paper (the temperature of the boiling water at the top and the lowest temperature you can read on the bottom). Draw a straight line on this paper and divide the line into equal divisions so that each line represents one degree Celsius of temperature. Attach the paper to the glass tube with cellophane tape.

Projects

1.   Measure the temperature of a room with your liquid thermometer. Compare your result with the temperature on a commercial thermometer. Find out if your liquid thermometer is more accurate at higher, lower, or midrange temperatures.

2.   Repeat the preceding project with your air thermometer. Compare the accuracy of your air thermometer with that of your liquid thermometer at all ranges of temperature.

3.   Design a science project that determines the relative advantages and disadvantages of gas and liquid thermometers.

4.   Galileo and Sanctorius did not have commercial thermometers with which to calibrate their thermometers. Instead, they used some well-known temperatures: the boiling and freezing points of water (100° C and 0° C) and body temperature (37° C). Devise a method for calibrating one or both of your thermometers using only these three temperatures.

5.   Refer to Project 4 under "Water Clock." Repeat the ice cube experiment described there using one of your thermometers to measure temperatures in that project.

6.   Use one or both of your thermometers to find out how temperature affects a plant or animal. For example, how does the behavior of beetles differ at high and low temperatures? How does the rate of seed germination depend on temperature? You can use the insect collector described in Chapter 4 to

collect the beetles you need for this experiment. Be sure to work only with plants or invertebrates.

7. Consult a reference book about bimetallic thermometers and try to build one of these instruments from the description you find there.

ASTROLABE

An astrolabe is a device for locating planets and stars. Sailors, explorers, and other travelers have used astrolabes for hundreds of years. By finding out the location of various celestial objects, navigators can determine their location on the earth. For example, the vertical angle of the North Star above the horizon is the same as the person's latitude on the earth. By using an astrolabe to find the angle of the North Star, navigators can also learn their current latitude. This method is especially important at sea, where people have few other means of knowing their location. Using an astrolabe to determine location is also known as "shooting a star."

Photo 8 shows an old astrolabe.

Caution: **Never use an astrolabe to locate the position of the sun because looking directly at the sun can damage your eyes.**

Materials: piece of wood about 2 inches × 12 inches × 12 inches; scissors; heavy white cardboard, at least 12 inches square; large protractor; pencil or pen; glue; hammer; nails; thin (finishing) nail; piece of wood about 2 inches × 4 inches × 24 inches; straw; piece of wood about 1 inch × 2 inches × 12 inches; string, 18 inches long; fishing weight; magnetic compass.

Photo 8. An astrolabe built in 1575

Directions

Note: Letters in parentheses—for example, (A)—are keyed in to Figure 4.

1. Use the 2 inch × 12 inch × 12 inch piece of wood (A) as the base for the astrolabe.

2. With the scissors, cut out a 12-inch circle from the piece of heavy white cardboard (B). Use the protractor to mark off the circle in units of 15° each.

3. Glue the cardboard circle to the top of the base, as shown in the diagram.

[40]

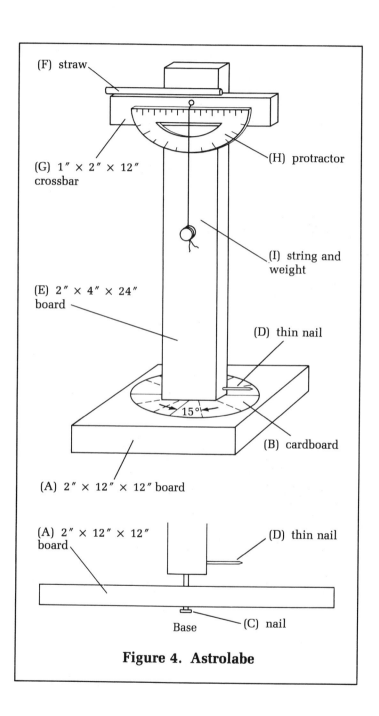

(F) straw

(G) 1″ × 2″ × 12″
crossbar

(H) protractor

(I) string and
weight

(E) 2″ × 4″ × 24″
board

(D) thin nail

15°

(B) cardboard

(A) 2″ × 12″ × 12″ board

(A) 2″ × 12″ × 12″
board

(D) thin nail

Base

(C) nail

Figure 4. Astrolabe

4. Hammer a nail (C) through the center of the base. This nail will act as a support for the vertical stand that holds the pointer.

5. Hammer the thin nail (D) into the narrow side of the 2 inch × 4 inch × 24 inch piece of wood (E) at a distance of about 2 inches from one end of the board. This nail will act as a pointer on the astrolabe.

6. Glue the straw (F) to one edge of the 1 inch × 2 inch × 12 inch board, the crossbar (G).

7. Glue the protractor (H) to the crossbar, as shown in the diagram.

8. At the end opposite the location of the "pointer" nail, nail the crossbar (with straw and protractor attached) to the wide side of the 2 inch × 4 inch board.

9. Work the crossbar back and forth a number of times until it moves easily on the vertical stand.

10. Hammer the stand onto the nail protruding from the base. Rotate the stand back and forth until it pivots easily on the nail.

11. Hang the string and weight (I), which serves as a plumb line, to the nail on the crossbar. Always checks this plumb line to be sure that the astrolabe is level before using it.

Sighting the North Star

On a clear evening, set up your astrolabe outdoors on a table or level piece of ground. Use the plumb line to be sure the instrument is level. The plumb line will hang straight down when the astrolabe is on level ground. Use the compass to point the 0° mark on the astrolabe to the north, as shown on the compass. Rotate the crossbar up and down until you can see the North Star by looking through the end of the straw. Read the angle of elevation (the angle of the North Star above the earth's horizon) on the protractor. The elevation of the North Star above the horizon is equal to your present latitude above or below the equator. You can use this information in building the sundial described after this project.

Additional Projects

1.   Select some other object in the night sky to observe. You can choose a star, a planet, or the moon. Determine the angular displacement of this object by rotating the vertical stand to the left or right of true north. Then determine the angle of elevation for the object as you did when you sighted the North Star.

2.   Measure the horizontal and vertical angles for any one star (except the North Star) every night for at least one month. Make a graph that shows the position of this star during the period of observation. Repeat this procedure for any one planet or for the moon.

3.   Locate the horizontal position of the moon as it rises or sets every day for at least one month. Measure the moon's position when it is always in the same vertical position, never more than a few degrees above the earth's horizon. Make a graph of your results.

SUNDIAL

Early cultures believed that the sun revolved around the earth. They knew that the sun's movement was very regular and were able to create a system for measuring time, based on the sun's position in the sky each day. This system used a sundial, one of the oldest devices for measuring time.

Over a period of many years, people developed improved forms of the sundial. But no sundial could measure time with an accuracy much better than about 15 minutes. Today, a sundial can still be used to measure long periods of time, to tell approximately what time of day it is, and to track the apparent motion of the sun across the sky.

Materials: felt-tip pen; rectangular piece of wood about 18 inches long and 12 inches wide; ruler; thin piece of metal about 12 inches long and 10 inches wide; tin snips; hammer and nail or drill bit; screwdriver; ¾-inch wood screws; spirit level; magnetic compass; clock or watch.

Directions
Note: Letters in parentheses—for example, (A)—are keyed in to Figure 5.

1.   Use the felt-tip pen to draw a circle (A) on the piece of wood. The center of the circle should be at the center of the board, and the circle should have a diameter of about 6 inches.

2.   Bend the long side of the metal piece (B) at a point about 1 inch from the edge. A right angle will be formed between the small part and the main part of the metal piece. The result will look like Figure 5, Side View of Metal Piece.

3.   With the pair of tin snips (careful!), cut the metal piece in such a way that angle XYZ in the

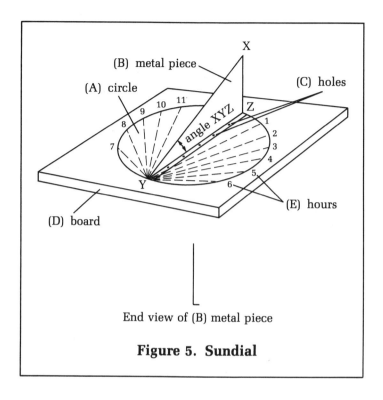

End view of (B) metal piece

Figure 5. Sundial

diagram is equal to the latitude where you live. For example, if the latitude of your city is 42°, the angle XYZ should be cut to 42°. (You can round off the measurement to the nearest degree.) You can find your city's latitude on maps published by the U.S. Geological Survey, or check at your local library.

4. With the hammer and nail or a drill bit, make one hole (C) in the narrow edge of the metal piece. Then make four more.

5. Use the screwdriver to attach the piece of metal (called the gnomon) to the wooden board (D) with the screws. The long side of the gnomon

[45]

should be parallel to and midway between the two long sides of the board.

6. Place the sundial on a perfectly flat surface. Use the spirit level to make sure the sundial is completely horizontal. With the aid of the compass, arrange the sundial so that the gnomon points directly at the north.

7. With the felt-tip pen, mark off each hour (E) on the circle by noting the location of the gnomon's shadow on the wooden board. Use the clock or watch and make your markings at each hour, from daybreak to sunset.

Projects

1. Suppose you wanted to hang your sundial on a wall. What changes would you have to make to use it in this position?

2. Do the dimensions of your sundial make any difference in the accuracy of this instrument? Find out whether or how the sundial's accuracy is affected by making the gnomon larger or smaller.

3. The sundial is really a way of tracking the sun's apparent motion in the sky. Make use of this concept to find a way of tracking the sun's daily motion over a period of one month.

4. The sun travels once around the sky, through a distance of 360°, every 24 hours. That means that the sun moves a distance of about 15° (360° ÷ 24) every hour. Think of a way of modifying your sundial to see if you can observe this pattern. How can you explain any differences (if any) between the pattern you expected and the one you observed?

5. Model the sun's movement with a flashlight. Place the sundial in a dark room and use the flash-

light to represent the sun. Move the flashlight around the sundial as you think the sun moves across the sky. Make records of the shadows cast by the sundial when the sun moves low in the sky, when it moves high in the sky, and when it moves in some intermediary path. Decide which time of the year is represented by each of the records you make.

6.   What would shadows cast by the sundial look like at (1) the North Pole, or (2) the equator during various times of the year? Use the modeling technique described in Project 4 to answer these questions.

SPRING BALANCE

A balance is a device for finding the weight of an object. Scientists use many types of balances. Some are suitable for measuring very small weights, others for determining larger weights. The balance described here can be adapted to measure a relatively wide variety of weights, from quite small to quite large. Once you have built this balance, you will be able to use it in other science projects. You can also use it around the house for weighing quantities in the kitchen. Photos 9 and 10 demonstrate the evolution in balance technology.

Materials: wooden board 1 inch × 2 inches × 12 inches; wooden board 2 inches × 4 inches × 6 inches; screwdriver; wood screws; glue; stiff white paper, at least 2 inches × 12 inches; hammer; two nails; masking tape; ruler; heavy steel spring about 6 inches long; three pieces of steel wire, about 4 inches long each; small aluminum pie pan; cardboard or yardstick or meter stick; mass units ("weights").

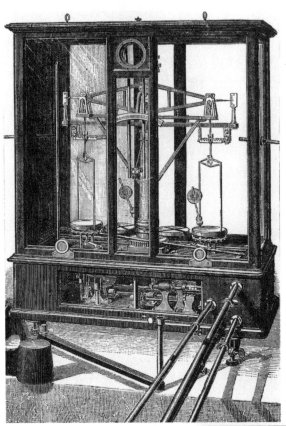

PHOTO 9.
An old double-pan
balance

PHOTO 10.
A modern digital balance

Directions

Note: Letters in parentheses—for example, (A)—are keyed in to Figure 6.

1.   Attach the 1 inch × 2 inch × 12 inch board (A) to the 2 inch × 4 inch × 6 inch board (B) with two screws inserted from the bottom of the 2 inch × 4 inch × 6 inch board.

2.   Glue the piece of stiff white paper (C) to the front of the vertical board. The paper will be used for the scale on your balance.

3.   Hammer the nail (D) into the vertical board about 2 inches from the top.

4.   Wrap a piece of the masking tape (E) around the nail a few times, about ¼ inch from its head. The tape will hold the spring in place on the nail, preventing it from sliding back and forth.

5.   Hang the spring (F) from the nail.

6.   With the hammer and second nail, punch three small holes around the edge of the pie pan (G). Pass one of the 4-inch lengths of steel wire through each hole. Bend the wires (H) up to form hooks that will hold the pan. Twist the tops of the wires together so that they can be hooked over the end of the spring.

Calibrating Your Balance

Now your balance is ready to calibrate. Find the position where the balance pan hangs when it is empty. Draw a line on the white paper that corresponds to this position. Mark the line with a zero (0). This position on the scale is called the "zero point" for your balance. Use care when marking the zero point. Place a piece of cardboard or yard-

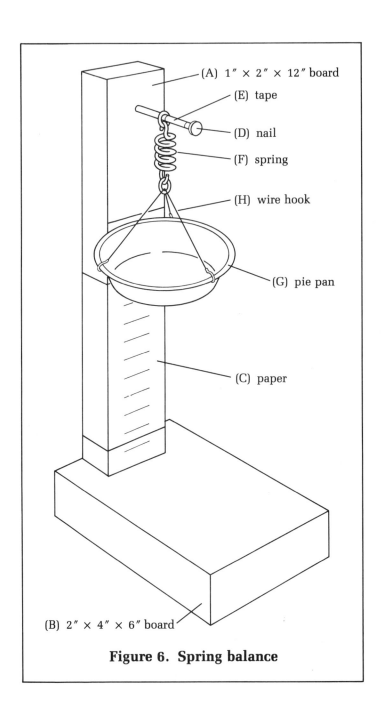

(A) 1″ × 2″ × 12″ board

(E) tape

(D) nail

(F) spring

(H) wire hook

(G) pie pan

(C) paper

(B) 2″ × 4″ × 6″ board

Figure 6. Spring balance

stick or meter stick under the pan to show exactly the place on the paper where the zero point line should be drawn.

Borrow a set of mass units ("weights") from a science teacher. Place a 50-gram mass on the balance pan and see where the pan hangs. Mark that position on the scale with a line and label the line "50 grams." Again, use care that the line exactly corresponds with the bottom of the balance pan. Repeat this process with mass units of 100 grams, 150 grams, 200 grams, etc.

An important caution to keep in mind is that every metal spring has an elastic limit. The elastic limit of a spring is the greatest amount the spring can be stretched and still have it return to its original length. Every time you remove a set of mass units from the balance pan, check to see if the pan returns to the zero point. If it does not, the spring has exceeded its elastic limit and it cannot be used to measure masses this large. You will then have to replace the spring with a new spring to continue using this balance.

Projects

1.   Test the accuracy of your balance by weighing a number of objects on it and then on a laboratory balance. Make any changes that you can think of that will make your balance more accurate.

2.   Think of changes that could be made in your balance that would allow you to find the weight of fairly heavy or very light objects.

3.   Another type of balance can be made with a rubber band rather than a spring. Construct such a balance and determine the relative advantages and disadvantages of each type of balance.

4.   Repeat Project 2 with your rubber band balance.

5.   You can use your balance to make the weighings needed in a number of simple physical, chemical, and biological projects. For example, find out how the rate of evaporation changes. Get a glass jar that will fit on the pan of your scale. Clean and dry the jar and weigh it as accurately as possible. Fill the jar with water and weigh the jar and water. Set the jar aside where it will not be disturbed. Do not cover it. Weigh the jar and water an hour later. Repeat this process every hour from early in the morning to late in the day. Make a graph that shows the changes in weight that occur. Since all the water will probably not evaporate in one day, try repeating the project by weighing the jar and water every 12 hours until the water is all gone. What factors affecting the rate of evaporation could you test in other projects?

6.   Consult a life, earth, or physical science laboratory book to find other projects in which balances are used. See how well your balance works on one or more of these projects.

WATER TEMPERATURE GAUGE

Many people think of lake, ocean, or river water as being "warm" or "cold." But scientists know that water temperatures can differ considerably at various depths and at various locations in the same body of water. A water temperature gauge will allow you to determine the temperature at any point in any body of water.

One use of a water temperature gauge is in studying thermal (heat) pollution. Industries often use water from lakes and rivers to cool machines or chemical reactions in their plants. When that water is returned to the lake or river, it is likely to be warmer than it was originally. Heated water can cause both harmful and beneficial effects on aquatic plants and animals.

Materials: fishing line; tape measure; scissors or tin snips; window screen, about 6 inches × 12 inches; outdoor or scientific thermometer; wire; fishing weight.

Directions

Note: Letters in parentheses—for example, (A)— are keyed in to Figure 7.

1.   Begin with a length of fishing line that you think will reach to the bottom of the body of water you have chosen to study.

2.   Tie knots (A) in the line at intervals of about 1 foot. The knots will let you know how much line is under water.

3.   Being careful not to cut yourself, cut a piece of window screen to fit snugly around the thermometer. Wrap the screen (B) around the thermometer (C) and hold it in place with two pieces of wire wrapped around it.

4.   Tie the thermometer to one end of the fishing line. Attach the heavy fishing weight (D) to the line directly above the thermometer.

Measuring the Temperature of a Lake or Pond Bottom

Select a body of water (lake, pond, swimming pool, stream, or river) that is more than three feet

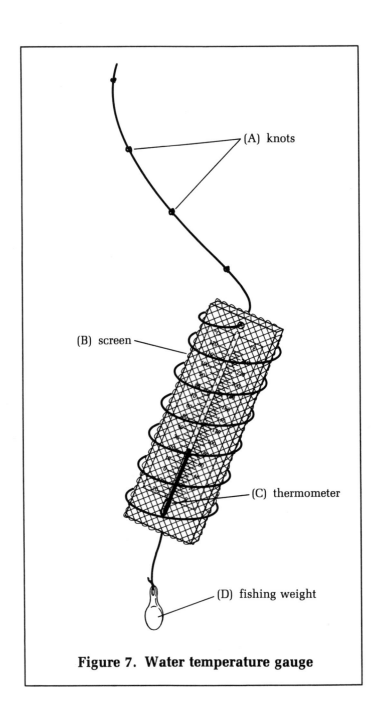

(A) knots

(B) screen

(C) thermometer

(D) fishing weight

Figure 7. Water temperature gauge

deep. Lower the water temperature gauge into the body of water until it touches bottom. Leave the thermometer on the bottom for 3 minutes. Pull up the thermometer, read, and record the water temperature. *Caution:* **Make sure that an adult partner accompanies you anytime you work in or near a body of water.**

Additional Projects

1.   Find a body of water at least 6 feet deep. Measure the temperature of the water at depths of 1 foot, 2 feet, 3 feet, and so on, to the maximum depth of the water. Make a graph of your results.

2.   Locate a lake or pond whose water is used for cooling by a local industry. Do a study of temperatures at various depths and in various locations throughout the body of water. Try to determine if thermal pollution exists in the water. Find out if the temperatures you determine are harmful to any forms of plant or animal life in the water.

3.   Do a complete temperature study of a small lake or pond. Determine the water temperature at various depths and in various locations throughout the body of water.

SECCHI DISK

One measure of water pollution is clarity. The more polluted a river, lake, or pond is, the murkier it may be. The less polluted it is, the clearer the water may be. Water that is not polluted may also be murky. For example, rivers and streams often become murky after a rainstorm.

A standard method for measuring the clarity of water is with a Secchi (pronounced SEK kee) disk, a circular piece of metal painted black and white. You drop the Secchi disk into a body of water until the distinction between white and black markings is no longer visible. The depth at which the disk can be seen—a measure of the water's clarity—is called the *limit of transparency* or *limit of visibility*. One way to use a Secchi disk is to measure the murkiness in lakes, ponds, rivers, and streams in your community.

Materials: scissors or tin snips; piece of aluminum sheeting, about ⅛ inch thick and at least 6 inches square; metal file; pencil; waterproof (oil-based) black paint; waterproof (oil-based) white paint; hammer; nail; two washers and nuts; eyebolt; fishing line; paper clip.

Directions
Note: Letters in parentheses—for example, (A)—are keyed in to Figure 8.

1.   Use the scissors or tin snips (careful!) to cut a circle about 6 inches in diameter out of the aluminum sheeting (A). Use the metal file to smooth or eliminate any sharp edges or corners. *Caution:* Always file with a motion away from your own body.

2.   With the pencil, divide the disk into four equal sections. Paint two opposite quarters black (B) and two opposite quarters white (C). Allow the paint to dry thoroughly.

3.   With the hammer and nail, make a hole (D) in the center of the metal disk.

4.   Hold one washer (E) and nut (F) on each side of the center hole as you thread the eyebolt (G) through the hole.

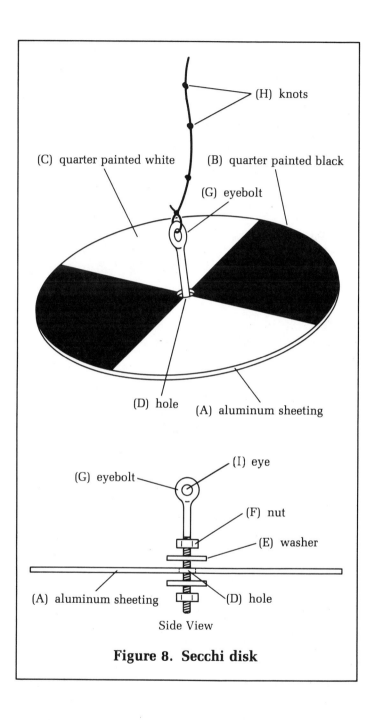

(H) knots

(C) quarter painted white   (B) quarter painted black

(G) eyebolt

(D) hole   (A) aluminum sheeting

(I) eye

(G) eyebolt

(F) nut

(E) washer

(A) aluminum sheeting   (D) hole

Side View

Figure 8. Secchi disk

5.   Tie knots (H) in the fishing line at intervals of about 1 foot.

6.   Attach the fishing line to the eye of the eye-bolt (I).

Murkiness Test of a Pond or Lake

Slowly lower the Secchi disk into a pond or lake. Watch for the point at which the disk disappears from view. Place a paper clip or make a knot on the fishing line to indicate this depth. Raise the disk slowly until it once again reappears. Place a second paper clip on the fishing line to indicate this depth. The limit of visibility is the average distance between the two points on the line. Repeat the process until you get the same reading twice for the limit of visibility.

Additional Projects

1.   Ask two or three friends to repeat the test above using the Secchi disk. Make a list of factors that might explain how results differ from person to person. Prepare a procedure that you can use every time that will eliminate human error as much as possible in using this device.

2.   Determine the limit of visibility for a river, lake, or other body of water at 1-hour intervals throughout the day. Make a graph that shows the results of these tests. Find out if the results you obtain are different for different times of the year.

3.   Determine the limit of visibility for any system of waterways you know of. A typical system is a pond or lake and the rivers and streams that flow into and out of it.

[58]

4.   Develop a hypothesis as to the factors that might affect the limit of visibility of a body of water over a period of 1 month. Then conduct a series of tests with the Secchi disk to test your hypothesis.

5.   Find a river, lake, or other body of water in your community that looks murky. Devise a project that will help you locate possible sources of this murkiness and changes in the amount of murkiness.

3

EQUIPMENT

FOR THE

EARTH SCIENCES

Most of the equipment described in this chapter is used in weather prediction. Weather prediction is still an inexact science. Meteorologists—people who study weather—know that moisture content of the air, winds, high- and low-pressure areas, temperature, and other factors are all involved in determining tomorrow's weather . . . or that of next week. But they are unsure as to how these factors interact. As a result, dependable weather forecasts can seldom be made for more than 24 hours in advance in most locations.

Unlike reliable weather forecasts, however, weather instruments are fairly easy to make and use. You can build a weather station that will give you good data of the kind meteorologists use in predicting the weather. In fact, one of the interesting things about building weather instruments is that you can make daily weather forecasts and compare your predictions with those of professional meteorologists as reported in newspapers and on television.

Two projects in this chapter deal with some simple characteristics of the earth around you. As you read about the clinometer and soil compaction gauge, you may think of other properties of the ground that you would also like to study.

BAROMETER

A barometer is a device for measuring air pressure. Since changes in air pressure often accompany weather changes, barometers are used in predicting weather patterns. Since air pressure changes with altitude, barometers can also be used to measure the distance above sea level. Altimeters in aircraft, for example, are essentially sophisticated modifications of a simple barometer.

Two common types of barometers exist, those that contain a liquid and those that do not. The latter type is called an aneroid barometer. The aneroid barometer described below can be used to measure changes in air pressure, which are an important clue to changing weather patterns.

Photo 11 shows an old aneroid barometer; Photo 12, an old mercury barometer; and Photo 13 (the right-hand instrument), a more modern (but still rather old-fashioned) aneroid barometer.

Materials: glue, two pieces of wood, 1 inch × 8 inches × 12 inches; pencil; stiff white cardboard, about 6 inches × 8 inches; sheet of thin rubber, such as a rubber dam used by dentists, large enough to cover the wide-mouth glass jar; wide-mouth glass jar, such as a pickle jar; two rubber bands or a piece of steel wire; insulating material,

[61]

Photo 11. An old aneroid barometer

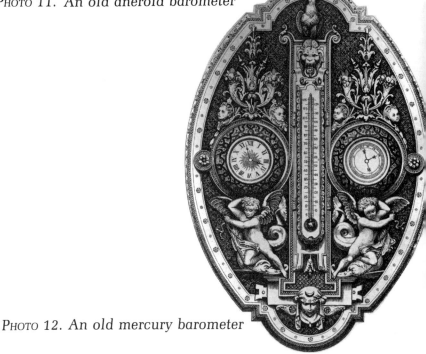

Photo 12. An old mercury barometer

PHOTO 13. A more recent barometer

such as plastic "bubble" sheet, Styrofoam, glass wool, etc., large enough to completely cover the wide-mouth glass jar; soda straw; scissors.

Directions

Note: Letters in parentheses—for example, (A)—are keyed in to Figure 9.

1.   Glue together the two pieces of wood (A) to make the stand shown in the diagram.

2.   With the pencil, make a scale on the white cardboard (B) with a line marked 0 in the middle and lines marked 1, 2, 3, etc., at equal distances above and below the line.

3.   Pull the rubber sheet (C) tightly over the mouth of the glass jar (D). Wrap the two rubber bands around the neck of the jar to hold rubber sheet in place. Alternatively, you can hold the rubber sheet in place by wrapping a wire around the neck of the jar and twisting the ends together to hold it in place.

4.   Wrap a layer of the insulating material (E) around the jar.

5.   Glue the soda straw (F) to the rubber sheet so that one end of the straw extends at least 3 inches beyond the edge of the jar. With the scissors, cut one end of the straw at an angle (G) so that it forms a pointer.

6.   Place the jar on the wooden base so that the straw pointer nearly touches the vertical board.

7.   Position the cardboard scale on the vertical board so that the 0 line (H) is level with the straw

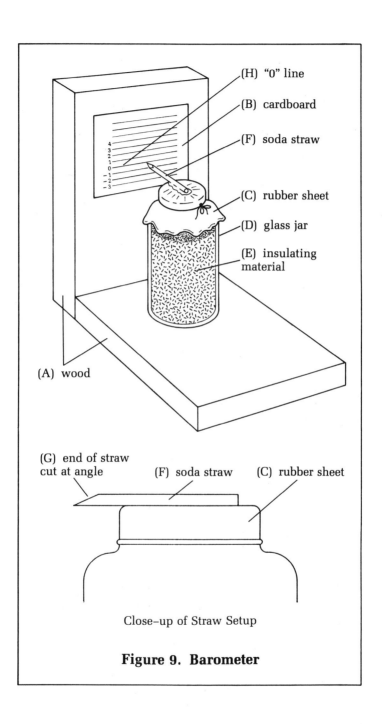

(H) "0" line

(B) cardboard

(F) soda straw

(C) rubber sheet

(D) glass jar

(E) insulating material

(A) wood

(G) end of straw cut at angle

(F) soda straw

(C) rubber sheet

Close–up of Straw Setup

Figure 9. Barometer

pointer. Glue the cardboard into position on the wooden board.

Measuring Changes in Barometric Pressure
Set your barometer someplace where it will not be affected by changes in temperature, such as away from windows or radiators. Observe changes in the straw pointer's position at regular intervals for 3 days. Make a graph of the results you observe.

Additional Projects
1.   Repeat the above activity for a period of 1 week. During the same time, keep a record of readings from a commercial barometer placed near your own barometer. Make a graph of the readings on both barometers. Compare the two graphs and evaluate the accuracy of your own barometer.

2.   Repeat the original activity for 1 week. Use the data collected each day to predict weather conditions on the following day. In a general sense, a falling barometer is associated with the approach of bad weather (rain and storms), while a rising barometer is associated with fair weather (clear skies). Assess the effectiveness of your barometer for purposes of weather prediction.

ANEMOMETER

An anemometer measures wind speed. In the form of anemometer described here, the wind pushes against four cups, making them revolve around a central pole. The faster the wind blows, the faster the cups revolve.

Anemometers are used in weather forecasting because they tell a meteorologist how rapidly a front is moving into an area. They are also used in aviation because pilots need to know the speed (as well as the direction) of winds as they take off, land, and plot their courses. You can use an anemometer to measure wind speed in your neighborhood. Then you can use this information, combined with other weather measurements, to try predicting tomorrow's weather.

Safety Note: Review the cautions in Appendix 1 about working with glass. Work under adult supervision and wear safety goggles and a lab coat or lab apron while working on this project. Use caution in working with flames.

Materials: hammer and chisel; two wooden sticks, 2 inches × 2 inches × 18 inches long; glue or thumbtacks; paint (any dark color); four cone-shaped plastic cups; glass tubing, at least 4 inches long; triangular file; pencil and ruler; glass tubing, at least 4 inches long; Bunsen or alcohol burner; drill or brace and bit; block of wood, 2 inches × 12 inches × 12 inches; wooden dowel to fit inside glass tubing; variable-speed electric fan; watch or clock that displays seconds.

Directions

Note: Letters in parentheses—for example, (A)—are keyed in to Figure 10.

1. To make the crossbars, use the hammer and chisel to notch the two wooden sticks (A) so that they will fit together at right angles. Glue the sticks together at the notch (B). Use *caution* in working with the chisel as the edge is very sharp.

2. Paint one of the four cups any dark color.

[67]

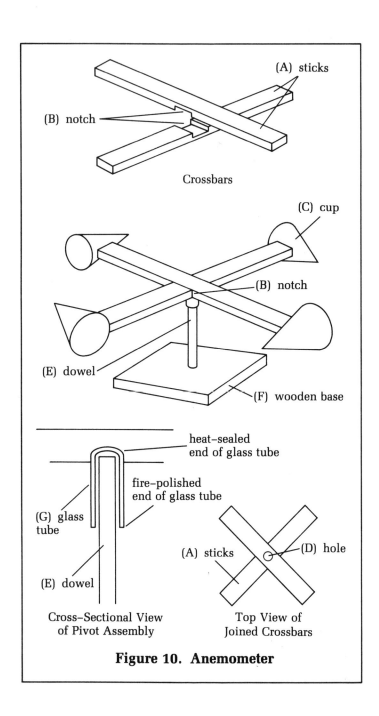

Figure 10. Anemometer

3.   Glue the four cups (C) to the ends of the cross-bars.

4.   Read the instructions in Appendix 1 about cutting and fire-polishing glass tubing. Cut a piece of the glass tubing about 4 inches long. Fire-polish one end of the glass tube. Heat-seal the opposite end.

5.   With a drill or brace and bit, drill a hole through the center of the wooden block to be used as a base for the anemometer. The hole should be just large enough to hold the wooden dowel snugly. Use *caution* in working with a drill or a brace and bit as the points on these tools are very sharp.

6.   With the drill or brace and bit, drill a hole (D) about halfway through the exact middle of the crossbar. The hole must be large enough to hold the glass tube.

7.   Fit the wooden dowel (E) into the wooden base (F). Place the glass tube upside down over the wooden dowel, as shown in the Figure 10 cross-sectional view (G). Place the crossbar over the top of the glass tube, as also shown in the cross-sectional view. Gently spin the crossbar to make sure it revolves smoothly.

Measuring Wind Speed

Set the anemometer about 3 feet in front of the variable-speed electric fan (*careful!*). Turn on the fan at its lowest speed. Observe the painted cup to count the number of times the crossbar makes one complete revolution in 1 minute. Increase the fan to its next highest speed. Count the number of revolutions per minute at this speed. Repeat for each speed available on the fan. Make any adjustments

[69]

in the anemometer to ensure that it revolves smoothly on the central pole. Record the wind speed in revolutions per minute. Project 2 below involves converting to miles per hour.

Additional Projects

1. Use the anemometer to measure the wind speed outside your home at regular intervals during the day. Record the highest and lowest speed in revolutions per minute.

2. You can calibrate your anemometer in one of two ways. First, you can borrow a commercial anemometer and calibrate your own anemometer against it. Second, you can have a friend drive you in a car traveling at exactly 5 miles per hour. Hold your anemometer out the window of the car and find out how many revolutions per minute it makes at this speed. Then increase the car speed to 10 miles per hour, 15 miles per hour, and 20 miles per hour. Do not try to calibrate the anemometer for speeds any faster than 20 miles per hour in the car.

3. Use your anemometer to find out what wind patterns are like around your home or school yard. How can you explain the patterns you observe?

4. Design a project to find out how bushes, trees, and other house plantings affect wind speed.

HAIR HYGROMETER

One material that is especially sensitive to changes in humidity is human hair. The term *humidity* refers to the amount of moisture in the air. When the moisture content of air increases, hair expands. As air becomes drier, hair contracts. This phenomenon is put to use in a measuring device known as a hair hygrometer. Hygrometers are useful in weather prediction because they tell a meteorologist what the humidity of the air is.

After you make the simple model described below, you may want to think about modifications that will make it more precise. (The left-hand gauge shown in Photo 13 is a hygrometer.)

Materials: hammer; nails; small nail; glue; wooden board, 2 inches × 8 inches × 8 inches; wooden board, 2 inches × 4 inches × 18 inches; wooden board, 2 inches × 2 inches × 4 inches; drill or brace and bit; wooden dowel about 6 inches long and thin enough to fit through spool; ruler; pencil or pen; two thin pieces of wood, 1 inch wide and 3 inches long; wooden or plastic spool; scissors; stiff white cardboard, about 6 inches square; modeling clay; human hair, at least 12 inches long, but longer, if possible; small fishing weight, of at least 1 ounce; towel.

Directions
Note: Letters in parentheses—for example, (A)—are keyed in to Figure 11.

1. Make a stand for the hygrometer by nailing or gluing the first three boards (A1, A2, A3) to each other as shown.

2. With the drill or brace and bit, drill a hole (B), large enough to hold the dowel, in each thin piece of wood (C) about 1 inch from one end of the wood.

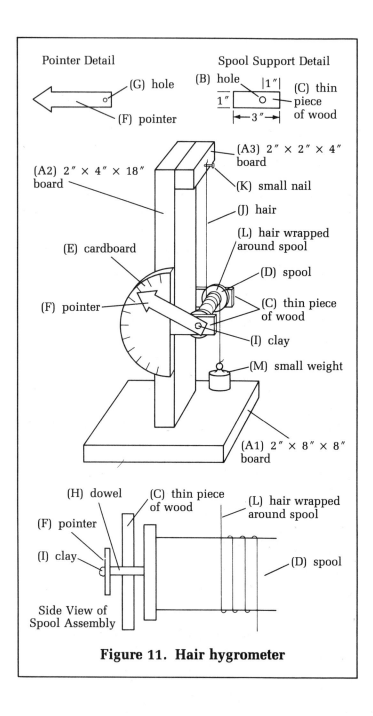

Figure 11. Hair hygrometer

3.   Glue or nail the thin pieces of wood to either side of the vertical board. These pieces will act as supports for the spool (D).

4.   With the scissors, cut out a semicircle, about 6 inches in diameter, from the cardboard (E). Make a scale on the outer edge of the cardboard. Do not place any numbers on this scale.

5.   Glue the cardboard semicircle to the vertical board of the support stand.

6.   With the scissors, cut out a pointer (F) 1 inch wide and 5 inches long of the shape shown from the white cardboard. With the hammer and a nail, punch a hole (G) through the end of the pointer. The wooden dowel must fit tightly through this hole.

7.   Run the dowel (H) through the hole in one support piece, through the spool, and through the hole in the other support piece, as shown in the cross-sectional view. Attach the pointer to the end of the dowel near the cardboard scale. Arrange the pointer so that it is nearly—but not completely—touching the scale.

8.   Attach a small lump of the clay (I) on each end of the dowel to prevent its coming out.

9.   The human hair you use must be long enough to reach from the top of the stand, around the dowel a few times, to the bottom of the stand. Make sure the hair is thoroughly clean and free of oils.

10. Wrap one end of the hair (J) around a small nail (K) and pound the nail into the small board (A3) at the top of the stand.

11. Wrap the other end of the hair around the

wooden spool two or three times (L). Loop the hair through the hook in the small fishing or other weight (M) and knot the hair around the hook.

Calibrating the Hygrometer

Place the hygrometer in a location where the humidity is 100%. You could put it in a shower that has just been used, or you could surround the hygrometer with a warm, wet towel. The highest point on the cardboard scale reached by the arrow should be marked "100%." Now place the hygrometer in a place where the humidity is close to 0%. Put it on top of a radiator or near a furnace vent. *Caution:* Do not place the hygrometer anyplace that it is hot enough to catch fire. Mark the lowest point of the arrow on the scale as "0%." Finally, divide the scale into twenty equal parts (each part = 5% change).

Projects

1.   Use your hygrometer to find the humidity in your room at home or in your schoolroom each day for a week. Make a graph of your results.

2.   Obtain a commercial wet- and dry-bulb hygrometer and repeat Project 1. Compare the readings you obtain on the commercial and homemade hygrometers. Determine the amount of error in the hair hygrometer.

3.   Devise a project to find out if readings obtained from the hair hygrometer can help predict the approach of rain, snow, or another form of precipitation.

4.   How, if at all, does wind speed affect humidity? In order to answer this question, use the anemometer described earlier, in combination with

the hair hygrometer, to measure these two factors over a period of one week.

5.   Some of the instruments in a weather station are usually enclosed in some sort of box to protect them from direct contact with rain, sunlight, and wind. Design an enclosure for your hair hygrometer that will provide this kind of protection, but that will still give a valid measure of humidity.

RAIN GAUGE

It might seem simple to make a rain gauge. Just set out a jar when it rains and measure the amount of water that collects as it rains. The problem with this approach is that the amount of rain collected is often less than a half inch and therefore difficult to measure directly. In addition, simply sticking a ruler into the rainwater that collects in a jar is not the most exact way of making this measurement.

The instrument described below is similar in design to those used in weather stations. Rain is collected in a funnel with a wide opening, deposited in a jar, and then measured in a measuring tube. A rain gauge is used to keep track of the amount of rain that falls in an area over a given period of time.

Materials: glue; pencil or pen; ruler, strip of white paper, about ½ inch wide and as long as the narrow glass jar; tall, narrow glass jar, such as an olive jar (this is the *measuring* tube); glass or plastic jar or tin can, about 4 inches in diameter and about 6 inches tall (this is the *collecting* jar); small handsaw; piece of wood 2 inches × 4 inches, about 3 feet long; piece of wood, 2 inches × 6 inches × 6 inches; hammer; nails (optional); three strong rubber (elastic) bands; glass or plastic funnel to fit tightly into collecting jar (their diameters must be the same); modeling clay.

Directions

Note: Letters in parentheses—for example, (A)—are keyed in to Figure 12.

1. Glue the strip of white paper (A) vertically on the outside of the measuring tube (B).

2. Pour water into the collecting jar (C) until it reaches a depth of exactly 0.5 inch. Measure as exactly as you can. Pour the water from the collecting jar into the measuring tube.

3. With the pencil, make a line (D) on the paper at the height of the water in the measuring tube.

4. Carefully measure the distance from the bottom of the measuring tube to the line you have just drawn. Use this distance to measure off equal spaces (E) above the line, to the top of the jar. Divide the distance between each pair of lines into fifths. The measuring tube is now calibrated in units of 0.1 inch.

5. With the small handsaw (*careful!*), cut one end of the 2 inch × 4 inch × 3 foot board (F) to a point as shown. Glue or nail the 2 inch × 6 inch × 6 inch board (G) to the longer board to make a platform for the collecting jar.

6. With the hammer, drive the support stand into the ground at a place where you want to measure rainfall. Make sure there are no obstructions to prevent rain from falling into the collecting jar.

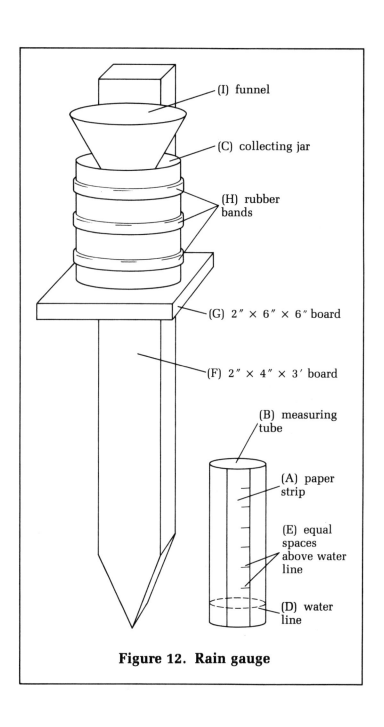

Figure 12. Rain gauge

Place the collecting jar on the stand and secure it to the vertical post with the rubber bands (H).

7. Place the funnel (I) into the mouth of the collecting jar. Secure the funnel in place with two or three small pieces of the modeling clay.

Measuring Rainfall

On a day when rainfall is expected, set out your rain gauge. After the rainfall, pour the water in the collecting jar into the measuring tube. Read off the amount of rainfall from the scale on the side of the tube.

Additional Projects

1. Ask your local weather service office for their records on a rainfall in your area, and compare those records with your own readings for the same rainfall. You can also obtain the information you need from newspapers at the library.

2. Find out if the amount of rainfall differs at various locations during the same storm.

3. Measure the amount of rainfall at various regular intervals during a storm. Make a bar graph that shows the amount of rainfall after 30 minutes, after 60 minutes, after 90 minutes, and so on.

SOIL COMPACTION GAUGE

A soil compaction gauge measures the extent to which soil can be compacted, or pushed down. Soil compaction depends on a number of factors, including the type of materials that make up the soil and the amount of moisture in the soil.

Information about soil compaction has a number of applications. For example, agricultural scientists can find out if a piece of land is suitable for growing crops. Soil that is very compacted usually retains little air. Plant roots find it difficult to obtain enough oxygen to grow properly. Heavily compacted soil also tends to hold moisture better than less compacted soil. Roots therefore may rot. With the information provided by a soil compactor gauge, an agricultural scientist or farmer will know whether land will have to be aerated or turned over before being ready for planting.

Materials: penknife; wooden dowel, 12 inches long, to fit inside spool; pencil; ruler; scissors; rubber band; spool used to hold sewing thread (usually made of pressed Styrofoam); steel wire; thumbtacks.

Directions
Note: Letters in parentheses—for example, (A)—are keyed in to Figure 13.

1. With the penknife, *carefully* sharpen one end of the wooden dowel to a point (A).

2. Draw a line (B) around the dowel about 1 inch from the point. This line will be the baseline for your gauge.

3. Starting about 1 inch from the unsharpened end of the dowel, draw lines (C) on the dowel downward at distances of 0.5 inch from each other. Number the lines downward 0, 1, 2, 3, and so on.

4. With the scissors, cut the rubber band (D) and fasten it loosely to the neck of the spool (E) with a piece of the wire (F).

[79]

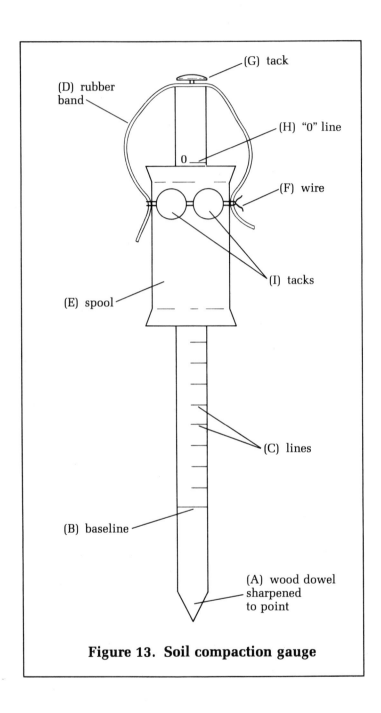

Figure 13. Soil compaction gauge

5.   Slip the spool over the dowel. Attach the rubber band to the top of the dowel with a thumbtack (G). Adjust the ends of the rubber band so that the top of the spool is level with the "0" line (H) on the dowel. Tighten the wire and secure the rubber band with thumbtacks (I).

Calibrating the Soil Compaction Gauge
Select a soil that you know to be very compacted and one that is not very compacted. Any grassy area is an example of the former, while the sand in a sandbox is an example of the latter. To use the gauge, hold the spool with one hand and push the gauge down gently into the soil. With each type of soil, push the pointed edge of the gauge into the soil up to the baseline. Observe the distance to which the rubber band is pushed upward. Read and record the line that corresponds to each type of soil. One number can represent "very compacted" soil on the scale, and the other number can represent "slightly compacted" soil on the scale.

Projects
1.   Estimate the amount of compaction in a variety of soils. Compare soil in a garden, a lawn, an open field, a hillside, a forest, and other locations. Make a bar graph that shows the degree of compaction for each soil tested.

2.   Hypothesize one specific factor that might influence the extent to which soil becomes compacted. Devise a project to test your hypothesis.

3.   Select one specific location to study. Determine the extent to which various amounts of water affect the compaction of soil in this location.

4. Hypothesize the association between soil compaction and plant growth. Devise a project to test your hypothesis.

CLINOMETER

A clinometer measures the slope of a hill. One use for such measurements is in the drawing of a topographic map. You can make a series of measurements with a clinometer at regularly spaced positions in an area and determine the contour of the land in that area. From this information, you can construct a topographic map of the area.

Materials: scissors; ruler; pencil; piece of heavy white cardboard, about 12 inches square; protractor; strip of wood, 1 inch × 2 inches × 16 inches; thumbtacks or glue; fishing weight, at least 1 ounce in weight; heavy string; soda straw.

Directions

Note: Letters in parentheses—for example, (A)— are keyed in to Figure 14.

1. With the scissors, cut a half circle out of the heavy piece of white cardboard (A). The half circle should have a diameter of about 12 inches.

2. Use the protractor to mark off a series of angles on the cardboard. Mark the angles $0°$, $5°$, $10°$, $15°$, $30°$, and $45°$ on both sides of the half-circle and $90°$ in the middle (B).

3. Attach the half circle to the strip of wood (C) using thumbtacks (D) or glue.

4. Tie the fishing weight (E) to the string (F) and attach the string to the center of the half circle

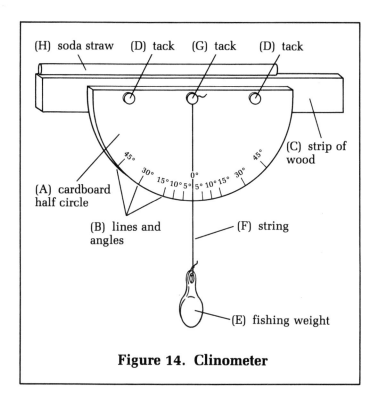

(H) soda straw   **(D) tack**   **(G) tack**   **(D) tack**

(C) strip of wood

(A) cardboard half circle

(B) lines and angles

(F) string

(E) fishing weight

Figure 14. Clinometer

with a thumbtack (G). The fishing weight should hang a few inches below the edge of the half circle.

5.　Glue the soda straw (H) along the top edge of the wooden support piece.

Finding the Slope of a Hill

Have a friend stand at the top of a hill. Point the clinometer toward your friend and look through the straw on the wooden support to get an exact sighting of her or him. Have a second friend read the position of the string on the half circle. This position gives you the slope of the hill.

[83]

Additional Projects

1.   Devise a plan to use your clinometer for measuring the contour of a piece of land near your home. Assuming that the lowest point on this piece of land is sea level (altitude = 0 feet), find a way to calculate the highest point of various hills on this land.

2.   Use your clinometer to measure the slope of a gully, valley, or other depressed area.

3.   Is the amount or type of vegetation on a hill related in any way to the slope of the hill? Devise a project that will allow you to answer this question.

4.   Is the amount of erosion on a hill related to its slope? Invent a method for answering this question (a) through a study of actual hills in your area and/or (b) by means of an experiment that you can carry out in your home or school laboratory.

5.   Locate three or more hills in your area that are bare of vegetation and that have different slopes. How, if at all, is the type of material at the base of each hill related to its slope?

6.   Can your clinometer be used to measure the altitude of various astronomical objects, such as stars, planets, and the moon? What adjustments, if any, do you need to make in order to use it for such purposes.

7.   What other applications can you think of for your clinometer? For example, could you use it to find the height of a building? Of what value would such a measurement have?

4
EQUIPMENT
FOR THE
LIFE SCIENCES

For many of us, plants and animals are the most interesting subjects of scientific research. We feel a special excitement about watching seeds sprout, measuring the growth of plants, or observing the behavior of fish or ants. You can design and build a range of scientific apparatuses that will help you make such observations.

However, equipment used in the life sciences often presents problems not encountered in other fields. This equipment may be used to capture or house living organisms. That means that you must use special care to design, build, and use this equipment in such a way as to avoid doing harm to the organisms. In no case should an instrument be used so as to injure or cause the death of an organism. Also, you should *never* use vertebrates in your animal studies. If you have any questions at all, be sure to talk with your adult partner about your project plans.

These conditions mean that you have to be

especially creative in building equipment for the life sciences. You may be able to think of modifications that will make a trap, cage, or other device both safer for an organism and more useful to you.

A SIMPLE MICROSCOPE

A microscope is an interesting tool to work with because it allows you to see structures and objects that may not be visible with the naked eye. For example, a drop of pond water may seem to be nothing but an empty speck of liquid to the naked eye. With a microscope, tiny organisms and bits of nonliving material come into view. Very complex, expensive microscopes make it possible to magnify objects thousands or millions of times, but you can easily make a simple microscope from inexpensive everyday materials. The most important part of your microscope is a simple lens. A lens is any transparent object that has a smooth, regular curvature. A drop of water or a small bead of glass will work as a lens in your instrument.

Like the telescope, the microscope has evolved a great deal over its history. The earliest microscopes had magnifications of only a few times; today's electron microscopes, of millions of times. Older microscopes could reveal cells; the newer ones can reveal individual molecules. Photos 14 and 15 show two early microscopes. Photo 16 shows a modern optical microscope. Photo 17 shows an electron microscope, which uses electrons instead of light to "illuminate" objects being observed.

Safety Note: Review cautions in Appendix 1 about working with glass. Work under supervision and wear safety goggles and a lab coat or lab apron. Use caution in working with flames.

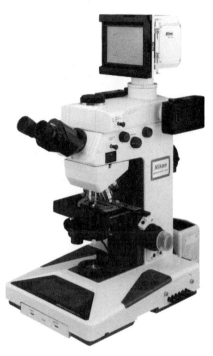

PHOTO 16.
A modern optical microscope

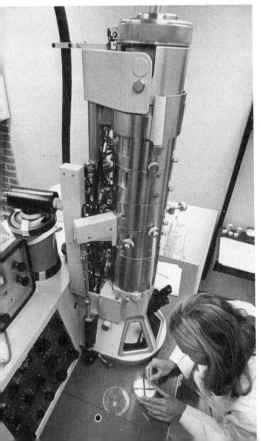

PHOTO 17.
An electron microscope

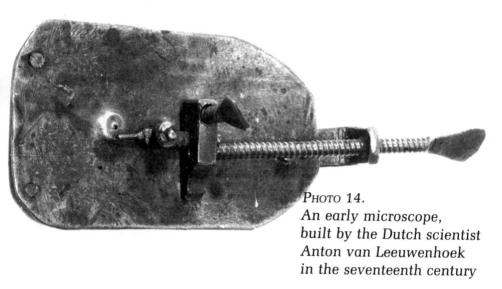

PHOTO 14.
An early microscope,
built by the Dutch scientist
Anton van Leeuwenhoek
in the seventeenth century

PHOTO 15. On the right is a model of the
microscope the English scientist Robert Hook
described in a book published in 1665.

Materials: strip of aluminum, about 6 inches × 2 inches; metal drill or hammer and nail; metric ruler; fine file; candle wax; piece of window glass, about 4 inches × 12 inches; two wooden blocks, about 4 inches × 4 inches × 2 inches; flat mirror, about 4 inches square; modeling clay or large eraser; medicine dropper (for water-drop lens); short (2–4 inch) solid glass tube, made of flint glass (for glass-bead lens); Bunsen or alcohol burner; glue; pot holders.

Directions

Note: Letters in parentheses—for example, (A)—are keyed in to Figure 15.

1. Make a hole (A) in the center of the aluminum strip (B) with the metal drill or hammer and nail. The hole should be about 2 millimeters in diameter. Use the metric ruler to measure the diameter of the hole.

2. With the fine file, remove all rough edges until the hole is as smooth as possible.

3. Bend the aluminum strip to form the lens mount (C). The bends should be made at a distance of about 2 inches from each end of the strip.

4. Melt a very small amount of candle wax (D) around the edge of the hole, on both sides of the aluminum strip. Do not let any wax get into the hole itself.

5. Place the piece of window glass (E) on top of the two wooden blocks (F). Then place the lens mount on top of the window glass. Support the mirror (G) below the lens mount with the piece of clay or large eraser (H). Use *caution* in working with the window glass. The edges may be sharp.

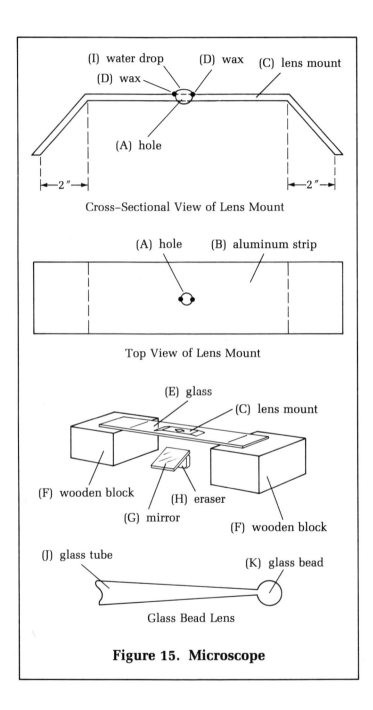

(I) water drop (D) wax (C) lens mount

(D) wax

(A) hole

|←—2″—→| |←—2″—→|

Cross–Sectional View of Lens Mount

(A) hole (B) aluminum strip

Top View of Lens Mount

(E) glass

(C) lens mount

(F) wooden block (H) eraser

(G) mirror

(F) wooden block

(J) glass tube (K) glass bead

Glass Bead Lens

Figure 15. Microscope

6.   To make a water-drop lens, use the medicine dropper to place a tiny drop of water (I) into the hole in the lens mount. You may have to experiment with various sizes and shapes of drops to see which one works best. The ideal shape seems to be one in which the top of the drop is somewhat flat and the bottom is elongated.

7.   To make a glass-bead lens:

  a. Read the instructions in Appendix 1 about cutting and fire-polishing glass tubing.

  b. Heat the solid glass tube (J) until it becomes very hot and soft. Use *caution* in heating the glass tube. Hold the tube with pot holders and do the heating only when your adult partner is present.

  c. Pull the glass rod from both ends to form a long, thin filament of glass.

  d. Allow the glass to cool; then break the filament in the middle.

  e. Reheat the end of one filament slowly and with constant turning. As the glass melts, it will form a bead (K) at the end of the filament.

  f. Continue heating with care until you have a bead of the desired size. The bead should be as round as possible and just small enough to fit into the hole of the lens mount.

  g. Attach the glass filament to the underside of the lens mount with a drop of glue. Do not let the glue get onto the glass bead itself.

8.   Objects to be viewed should be placed on the glass plate directly under the lens mount. You may have to adjust the shape of the lens mount in order to get the best possible image of the object being viewed.

Viewing a Drop
of Pond Water

With the medicine dropper, take a sample of water from a pond or lake or from an aquarium. Place a single drop of that water on the glass plate beneath the lens mount. Make a diagram of the objects you see with your microscope.

Additional Projects

1.   Place about 1 cup of pond water in a clean baby food jar and screw the cap tightly on the jar. Place a second sample of pond water in a second baby food jar and add 5 drops of milk to the jar. The milk serves as food for organisms in the jar. Screw the cap tightly on the second jar. Examine 1 drop taken from each jar at 1-day intervals for 1 week. Make diagrams that show any changes in each jar.

2.   Devise a project to determine the effect of other factors (such as heat or temperature) on organisms in your pond water sample.

3.   Determine the effect of a disinfectant or antiseptic on the organisms in your pond water. Use only 1 drop of the disinfectant or antiseptic to begin with; then see if larger amounts have different effects. You can use household-strength hydrogen peroxide, laundry bleach, or household ammonia. Make sure that your adult partner is with you when you use any of these materials.

POTOMETER

Green plants lose water from their leaves to the air in a process known as transpiration. A potometer is an instrument for measuring the rate at which this process occurs. As leaves lose water to the air, roots take up water from water within the potometer to replace the lost water. The potometer can be used to measure the effect of factors such as temperature, light, and leaf surface on the rate of transpiration.

Safety Note: Review the cautions in Appendix 1 about working with glass. Work under supervision and wear safety goggles and a lab coat or apron. Use caution in working with flames.

Materials: mayonnaise jar and cap; large nail; hammer; triangular file; pencil and ruler; glass tubing with an inner diameter of about ¼ inch, at least 12 inches long; Bunsen or alcohol burner; modeling clay; cellophane tape; plastic ruler or homemade scale; eyedropper; water colored with food coloring; large-leaved plant, such as a philodendron.

Directions
Note: Letters in parentheses—for example, (A)—are keyed in to Figure 16.

1.   Wash and dry the mayonnaise jar (A) and cap (B).

2.   Using the nail and hammer, make two holes in the cap large enough to hold the glass tube.

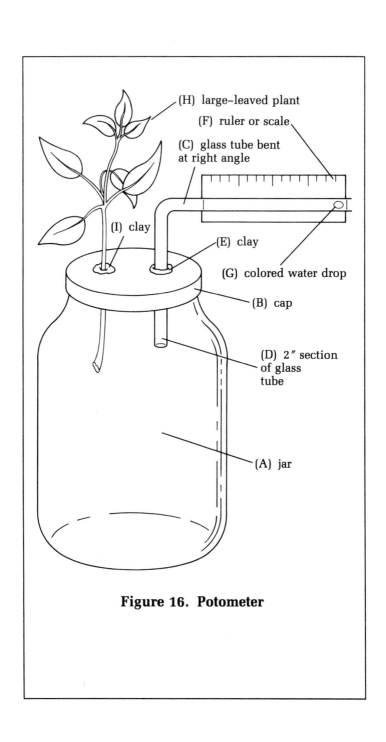

(H) large–leaved plant

(F) ruler or scale

(C) glass tube bent at right angle

(I) clay

(E) clay

(G) colored water drop

(B) cap

(D) 2″ section of glass tube

(A) jar

Figure 16. Potometer

3. Read the instructions in Appendix 1 about cutting and fire-polishing glass tubing. Cut and fire-polish the piece of glass tubing about 12 inches long.

4. Read the instructions in Appendix 1 about bending glass tubing. Have your adult partner assist or observe you when you make this bend. Bend the glass tubing at a right angle (C), as shown. The short section of the tube (D) should be about 2 inches long.

5. Insert the short end of the glass tube into one of the holes in the jar cap. Attach the tube to the cap with a small piece of the clay (E).

6. Attach the ruler or scale (F) to the long end of the glass tube using cellophane tape. You can make your own scale on a piece of cardboard.

7. Using the eyedropper, add a single drop of the colored water (G) to the open end of the glass tube. The drop should be as small as possible but large enough to completely seal the end of the tube.

8. Fill the jar with water and replace the cap on the jar.

Finding the Rate of Transpiration
Insert a cutting from the large-leaved plant (H) into the second hole in the cap. Hold the plant in place with a small piece of the clay (I). The clay must seal the cutting to the cap. As the plant takes up water, the droplet in the glass tube will move to the left. Find a way to calculate the rate at which the plant takes up water. You can use a unit of measurement such as cubic inches or milliliters per hour.

Additional Projects

1. Find out if or how light affects the rate of transpiration.

2. Determine how other factors (temperature, humidity, leaf size, number of leaves, etc.) might affect the rate of transpiration.

3. Compare the rate of transpiration for different types of plants. Keep in mind any factors that will have to be kept constant in making this comparison.

4. Compare the rate of transpiration for a plant cutting and for a rooted plant of the same kind.

5. This form of potometer can be used only until the water droplet in the horizontal glass tube passes all the way through the tube and into the jar. Modify this apparatus so that it can be used for a longer period.

INSECT COLLECTOR

Many types of insert collectors have been invented. The kind to make depends on the type of insect you want to capture. The collecting net described below is used to capture flying insects, such as butterflies, moths, and grasshoppers. After collecting an insect, you should release it or house it in a container that provides it with adequate space while you study it. Before you begin collecting, find out whether any rare or endangered species are likely to come your way. Do not catch any of these.

Materials: scissors; piece of cheesecloth, about 4 feet square; needle and thread; clothes hanger or a piece of heavy wire; broom handle; duct tape.

Directions

Note: Letters in parentheses—for example, (A)—are keyed in to Figure 17.

1.   Cut the piece of cheesecloth into the shape shown (A).

2.   Sew the two long sides and the smaller end of the cloth together to make a cone (B).

3.   Shape the closed part of the clothes hanger into a circle (C). Or make the circle of heavy wire.

4.   Wrap the curved end of the coat hanger or wire around the end of the broom handle (D). Secure the wire to the broom handle with duct tape (E).

5.   Wrap the open end of the cloth cone over the metal circle. Double-stitch the cloth around the wire to hold it securely in position.

Catching Flying Insects

One way to use your insect net is simply to try catching butterflies, moths, and other flying insects as they fly near you. Another method is to swing the net just above the ground. Insects caught by either method can be trapped simply by flipping the handle around once, sealing the open end of the net. Practice using your net *without* trying to capture insects before using it *with* insects.

Additional Projects

1.   Conduct a population survey of a field to see what kinds of insects can be found and how many of each live there.

2.   For a particular area, determine how the kinds and numbers of insects vary at various times of the day; at various times of the year.

[97]

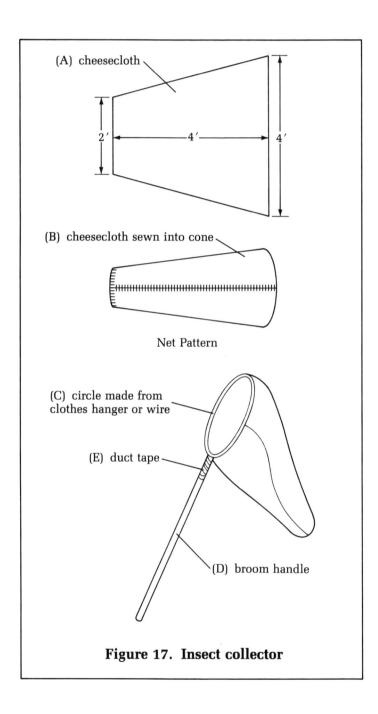

(A) cheesecloth

2′ ←——4′——→ 4′

(B) cheesecloth sewn into cone

Net Pattern

(C) circle made from
clothes hanger or wire

(E) duct tape

(D) broom handle

Figure 17. Insect collector

3. Find out how temperature, humidity, precipitation, and other weather conditions affect the numbers and kinds of insects found in a area.

4. Design a project that will allow you to determine what kinds of food certain flying insects like best.

5. Do the numbers and behaviors of insect populations differ at various times of the day? Design a project that will allow you to answer that question.

OBSERVATION CAGE

An observation cage is a narrow container fitted with glass on two sides. The cage is made narrow in order to let you see almost everything that occurs inside. If the cage is too narrow, the animals inside will not have room to move about and live normally. If it is too wide, you will not be able to observe some of the animals' projects. The cage described below is suitable for the observation of ants.

Materials: glue; two pieces of wood, 1 inch × 2 inches × 8 inches; one piece of wood, 1 inch × 2 inches × 12 inches; masking tape; two glass plates, ¼ inch × 10 inches × 12 inches, to fit the wooden frame; four wooden blocks, 2 inches × 2 inches × 4 inches; piece of wood, 1 inch × 1 inch × 12 inches.

Directions
Note: Letters in parentheses—for example, (A)—are keyed in to Figure 18.

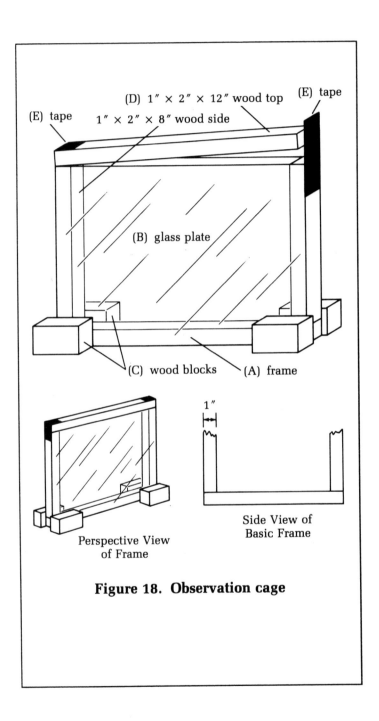

(D) 1″ × 2″ × 12″ wood top   (E) tape

(E) tape   1″ × 2″ × 8″ wood side

(B) glass plate

(C) wood blocks   (A) frame

1″

Perspective View
of Frame

Side View of
Basic Frame

Figure 18. Observation cage

1. Glue the two 1 inch × 2 inch × 8 inch pieces of wood to the top side (*not the ends*) of the 1 inch × 2 inch × 12 inch piece of wood to form a frame (A). The long piece of wood is the base; the shorter pieces, the sides.

2. When the glue has dried, tape one glass plate (B) to each side of the frame. Make sure the tape covers all exposed glass edges on the bottom and sides. Use *caution* in working with the glass plates. The edges may be sharp.

3. Glue the four blocks (C) to the bottom corners of the cage.

4. Place the 1 inch × 2 inch × 12 inch piece of wood (D) on top of the frame and attach it with two pieces of masking tape (E). When you need to remove the top, remove the masking tape from the sides of the frame.

5. Fill the cage to within 1 inch of the top with damp (not wet) soil. Add about twenty ants to the cage. Make sure that a queen ant is included. Talk with a biology teacher or pet store owner about the best kinds of ants to use. You may be able to purchase the ants at the pet store. Do *not* use carpenter ants.

6. Sprinkle small pieces of bread on top of the soil. Place the top on the cage.

Observing Ant Behaviors

Observe the ant cage for at least three days. Keep a record of the different ant behaviors you observe. Included among these behaviors might tunneling, contact with other ants, and feeding patterns.

Additional Projects

1.   Repeat the introductory activity with other ant species. Again, talk to a biology teacher or a pet store owner about other species to study. Find out if various species of ants demonstrate different kinds of behaviors.

2.   Devise an experiment that will determine the types of foods that ants do and do not prefer. Find out if the results of this experiment differ for various kinds of ants.

3.   Devise a series of experiments that will test other factors that might affect ant behavior. Such factors might include heat, light, and soil type.

4.   Adapt your ant observation cage for use with other soil-dwelling organisms (be sure to remove the ants first!) Worms are one possibility. Figure out what changes in the cage structure are needed to study worm behavior or that of some other organism that lives below ground.

5.   Your observation cage can also be used to study germination of seeds and root development in plants. Modify your cage so that it can be used for projects involving plants. Then design and carry out at least one such project.

5
EQUIPMENT
FOR THE
PHYSICAL SCIENCES

Equipment designed for physical science projects can be a fascinating introduction to the world of unseen phenomena. For example, the earth is flooded every day with radiation from outer space that humans cannot detect directly with their five senses. But you can easily build an instrument—the cloud chamber—that will reveal this radiation to you.

This equipment can also reveal a complexity in the natural world of which many people are not aware. A spectroscope is one of many instruments that analyzes something common and familiar—white light, in this case—and shows how much more complex it is than it seems to be.

Finally, many types of equipment can help you use simple physical phenomena to work for you. The telegraph set described in this section is a simple apparatus that uses electrical and magnetic fields to send messages across a distance.

ELECTROMAGNET

Electricity and magnetism are closely related. Every electric current generates a magnetic field, and changing magnetic fields can generate an electric current. These principles constitute the basis of many electrical appliances. Perhaps the simplest of all such devices is an electromagnet. An electromagnet consists of a solenoid—a coil containing many turns of wire—and an iron core. When an electric current passes through the solenoid, it generates a magnetic field around and within it. The magnetic field within the solenoid makes the iron core magnetic.

Materials: large machine bolt, at least 4 inches long, with nut to fit; scissors; pencil; ruler; white paper, as wide as the machine bolt is long and about 6 inches long; cellophane tape; no. 22 enamel or cotton-covered copper wire, about 10 feet long; 1½-volt dry cell; knife switch or doorbell button; magnetic compass.

Directions

Note: Letters in parentheses—for example, (A)—are keyed in to Figure 19.

1. Screw the nut (A) onto the end of the bolt (B).

2. Cut the piece of paper as wide as the bolt is long and to a length of about 6 inches. Wrap the paper (C) tightly around the bolt but not around the nut. Secure the paper with cellophane tape (D).

3. Starting next to the nut, carefully wrap the copper wire around the paper-covered bolt (E). Leave about 1 foot of wire free (F) at the beginning

[104]

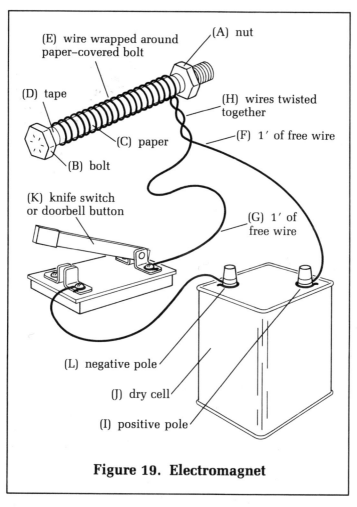

(E) wire wrapped around paper-covered bolt

(A) nut

(D) tape

(H) wires twisted together

(F) 1′ of free wire

(C) paper

(B) bolt

(K) knife switch or doorbell button

(G) 1′ of free wire

(L) negative pole

(J) dry cell

(I) positive pole

Figure 19. Electromagnet

of the coil. The wire should be tight around the bolt, and each loop should fit snugly next to those on either side. When you have threaded the end of the bolt, continue wrapping a second layer of coils, back toward the nut. Make sure you continue to wind in the same direction. When the second layer is complete, leave another foot of wire at the end (G).

[105]

4. Twist the two ends of wire together (H) so that the coils will not come loose from the bolt. The coiled wire in this device is the solenoid for your electromagnet.

5. Attach one end of the wire to the positive pole (I) of the dry cell (J). *Caution:* **Never use household current in this project.**

6. Attach the other end of the wire to the knife switch or doorbell button (K). Connect the other side of the switch or doorbell button to the negative pole (L) of the dry cell.

Testing Your Electromagnet

Activate your electromagnet by closing the switch. Bring the compass near each end of the electromagnet. Determine which end is a north-seeking pole and which is a south-seeking pole. *Hint:* Like magnetic poles attract each other; unlike poles repel. Do not leave the switch closed long or the dry cell will quickly run down.

Additional Projects

1. Map the magnetic field around your electromagnet. Support a piece of window glass about 8 inches square on four wooden blocks. Slide the electromagnet under the glass. Sprinkle iron filings evenly on top of the glass. Turn on the electromagnet and observe the pattern produced by the iron filings. The pattern can be better defined by tapping lightly on the edges of the glass. *Caution:* **Do not inhale the iron filings. Do not stir up the filings so as to create dust.**

2. Determine the strength of your electromagnet. Find out how many paper clips in a row the electromagnet can pick up when it is turned on.

3.   Your electromagnet will attract only materials that contain iron, cobalt, or nickel. Use your electromagnet to test common metallic objects in your home to see which ones contain one or more of these elements.

4.   Find out how increasing or decreasing the number of turns of wire on the solenoid affects the strength of your magnet.

5.   What is the effect, if any, of reversing the windings on the bolt?

6.   How is the strength of an electromagnet related to the voltage applied to it? You can answer that question by connecting additional batteries to each other in series. Ask your adult partner to show you how batteries are connected in series. Then design a project to answer this question.

7.   Devise a practical application for your electromagnet in your own home.

TELEGRAPH SET
One of the earliest devices for using electricity and magnetism for communications was the telegraph. A telegraph makes use of an electromagnet to produce temporary connections between two pieces of metal. When the two pieces come into contact, they make a *click* sound. When they lose contact, one piece of metal snaps back into its original position, striking a third piece of metal. The return snap produces a second click. When a telegraph operator touches the telegraph key briefly, the two clicks come in quick succession. The sound is known as a "dot" in international Morse code. If the key is held down a bit longer, the two clicks occur farther apart, producing a "dash."

Materials: two pieces of wood, 6 inches square; hammer and nails, or glue, or screwdriver and screws; electromagnet, commercial or homemade; clamps to hold electromagnet or two strips of copper, about 1 inch × 3 inches; strip of tin can, about ½ inch × 3 inches (*note:* any thin metal strip can be used as long as it contains iron; a "tin" can is made of iron or steel that has a thin coating of tin on it); drill; small right-angle bracket; pliers or wrench; bolt and nut to fit bracket hole; ¾-inch wood screw; paper clip; enamel or cotton-covered copper wire; 1½-volt dry cell; doorbell button.

Directions

Note: Letters in parentheses—for example, (A)— are keyed in to Figure 20.

1.   Attach the two pieces of wood (A) as shown, with nails, screws, or glue.

2.   Attach the electromagnet (B) to the vertical board using clamps or narrow strips of copper (C). If you use copper strips, attach them to the vertical board with screws.

3.   Drill a ¼-inch hole in one end of the "tin" strip (D). Attach the strip to the bracket with the bolt and nut (E).

4.   Attach the bracket to the back wooden panel with a screw (F). Locate the bracket so that the metal strip is no more than ⅛ inch from the electromagnet.

5.   Cut and bend the paper clip (G) so that it has the shape shown.

6.   Attach the paper clip to the back panel with a

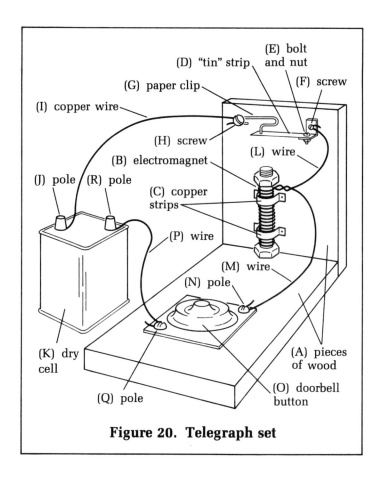

Figure 20. Telegraph set

screw (H). Locate the paper clip so that it is just barely touching the metal strip.

7.   To the same screw that holds the paper clip, attach a piece of copper wire about 20 inches long (I). Attach the opposite end of the wire to one pole (J) of the dry cell (K). *Caution:* **Never use household current in this project.**

8.   Attach one end of the wire (L) from the electromagnet to the bracket.

[109]

9. Connect the other end of the wire (M) from the electromagnet to one pole (N) of the doorbell button (O). Complete the circuit with a wire (P) between the second pole (Q) of the button switch and the second pole (R) of the dry cell.

Using the International Morse Code
Practice making dots and dashes by pressing the button switch (or doorbell) quickly and slowly. Have a friend confirm your ability by telling you when he or she can clearly tell the difference between a dot and a dash.

Additional Projects
1. The international Morse code is given in the table. Use this code to tap out your name on the telegraph.

THE INTERNATIONAL MORSE CODE

A • —	N — •	• • • • • •
B — • • •	O — — —	, • — • — • —
C — • — •	P • — — •	? • • — — • •
D — • •	Q — — • —	1 • — — — —
E •	R • — •	2 • • — — —
F • • — •	S • • •	3 • • • — —
G — — •	T —	4 • • • • —
H • • • •	U • • —	5 • • • • •
I • •	V • • • —	6 — • • • •
J • — — —	W • — —	7 — — • • •
K — • —	X — • • —	8 — — — • •
L • — • •	Y — • — —	9 — — — — •
M — —	Z — — • •	0 — — — — —

---

[110]

2.   Find a friend who is interested in learning Morse code with you. Take turns tapping out messages to each other on your telegraph.

3.   For additional projects involving your telegraph set, see Leon R. Stanley's *Easy to Make Electric Gadgets*, listed in the Bibliography.

PINHOLE CAMERA

The purpose of any camera is to capture the light rays that reflect off an object and focus those light rays on a piece of photographic film. Commercial cameras use lenses to make sure that light rays are focused properly on the film so that a sharp picture is obtained.

A simple method for obtaining a sharp, clear picture in a camera is to provide a very small opening, or aperture, for light rays to pass through. The pinhole camera described below is such a device. The clarity of your photographs will depend largely on how carefully you can make a tiny hole with clean edges for the aperture.

Materials: black spray paint or paintbrush and black paint or glue and black construction paper to fit inside cardboard box; ruler; pencil; cardboard box, about 5 inches × 5 inches × 5 inches, with a tight-fitting lid; aluminum foil, about 1 inch square; straight pin; Post-it or other self-stick paper, about 2 inches square; masking tape; film.

Directions
Note: Letters in parenthesis—for example, (A)—are keyed in to Figure 21.

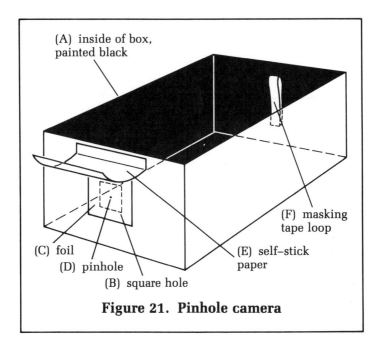

(A) inside of box, painted black

(F) masking tape loop

(C) foil

(D) pinhole

(E) self–stick paper

(B) square hole

Figure 21. Pinhole camera

1.   Paint the inside of the cardboard box and lid black (A), or glue the black construction paper to the inside walls and the inside of the lid.

2.   Cut out a square hole (B), ½ inch on a side, in one side of the box. Tape a piece of aluminum foil (C), 1 inch on a side, over the hole on the inside of the box.

3.   Use the straight pin to make a small hole (D) in the center of the aluminum foil.

4.   Cut a piece of the Post-it or other self-stick paper 1 inch wide and 2 inches long. Tape the paper (E) on the nonsticky end above the aperture so that it completely covers the hole in the box. Push the sticky end of the paper against the box to close the aperture.

5. Make a loop from 5 inches of masking tape, sticky side out. Attach the loop (F) to the inside wall of the box opposite the aperture. Press the loop against the box so that it is as flat as possible.

Making a Photograph

The camera must be loaded in a photographic darkroom or some other place where the lowest possible level of light is maintained. Obtain a piece of unexposed photographic film. Attach the film to the masking tape holder inside the box. The shiny side of the film should face toward the aperture. Place the lid on the box and close the paper cover. The lid must fit the box very tightly. If necessary, seal the lid to the box on all four sides with masking tape.

To take a picture, place the camera on a table or other flat surface and point it at the object you want to photograph. Remove the paper covering from the aperture for about 15 seconds. The time needed for the exposure will differ with the type of film you use and the brightness of the scene being photographed. Ask someone who works at a camera store to help you choose the film and help you determine the best exposure time.

Replace the paper covering and remove the exposed film inside a darkroom. Wrap the exposed film in black construction paper and seal the paper. Have a photographic shop or amateur photographer develop the photograph for you. (You may want to have this film developed along with other film used for the Additional Projects.)

Additional Projects

1. Repeat the exercise above using different exposure times. Keep all other conditions (light, in-

tensity, object photographed, distance from object to camera, etc.) the same. Find out the exposure time that gives the best results for these conditions.

2.   Find out how changing the distance between the camera and the object being photographed affects the clarity of your pictures.

3.   Vary the light source used with your camera by taking photographs in direct sunlight at various positions around the object, in indirect sunlight, and in artificial light.

4.   Find out how sunlight affects the growth of a seedling. Place one or more seedlings in a place where they will get sunlight from early morning until late afternoon. Take a picture of the seedling once each hour from sunrise to sunset. Make sure you place your camera in exactly the same place every time you take a photograph. How does the seedling's appearance change during the day?

5.   Design other science projects in which you can use pictures taken with your pinhole camera. A few ideas include the following:

a. Record the growth of a plant each day over a period of two weeks.

b. Make photographs of different types of clouds.

c. Use an anemometer (see Chapter Three) and the camera to make a scale that shows how much winds of various speeds affect the way a flag flies.

d. Measure the rate (with photographs) at which a nail rusts.

6. Try making photographs with your camera at night. What exposure time is needed to get a usable photograph? What can you learn from a photograph taken with an exposure time of 1 hour or more?

SPECTROSCOPE

A spectroscope is an instrument for breaking light up into its component parts. For example, white light consists of a whole range of colored light, ranging from red, orange, and yellow to green, blue, indigo, and violet. White light that passes through a spectroscope is divided into discrete bands having these colors. Light of colors other than white is also subdivided by a spectroscope into discrete colored bands or lines. The pattern of colored bands or lines that make up light is called a spectrum.

Some spectroscopes use a triangular piece of glass called a prism to break up light into its components. Other spectroscopes use a replica grating, a thin piece of plastic on which many fine lines are etched very closely to each other. The spectroscope described below uses a replica grating.

One application of the spectroscope is in astronomy. The light produced by a star is analyzed with a spectroscope to find out what elements and compounds occur in the star.

Safety Note: Use care when handling the knife or single-edged razor blade and the double-edged razor blade. Do not attempt to break the double-edged blade yourself, but ask your adult partner for assistance. Any object with a very sharp edge can be substituted for the double-edged razor blade.

[115]

Materials: replica grating; sharp knife or single-edged razor blade; ruler; shoe box; masking tape; double-edged razor blade, broken in half; fluorescent lamp.

Directions

Note: Letters in parentheses—for example, (A)—are keyed in to Figure 22.

1. Obtain a piece of replica grating at least 1 inch long from a science teacher or scientific supply company (see Appendix 2).

2. With the sharp knife or *single-edged* razor blade, carefully cut a viewing hole (A) about 1 inch in diameter in the middle of one end of the shoe box.

3. Use masking tape to attach the piece of replica grating (B) over the hole, on the inside of the shoe box. The lines of the grating should be perpendicular to the bottom of the shoe box. You may need help lining up the diffraction grating properly.

4. With the sharp knife or single-edged razor blade, cut a narrow slit (C) 1 inch long and no more than ¼ inch wide at the opposite end of the shoe box. The slit should be perpendicular to the bottom of the shoe box. It should also line up with the viewing hole at the opposite end of the box.

5. Attach the two halves of the *double-edged* razor blade (D) to the sides of the slit. Your objective is to make the slit as narrow as possible by lining up the razor blade edges as closely as possible. But do not let the two edges actually touch. Fasten the razor blade pieces to the outside of the shoe box with masking tape.

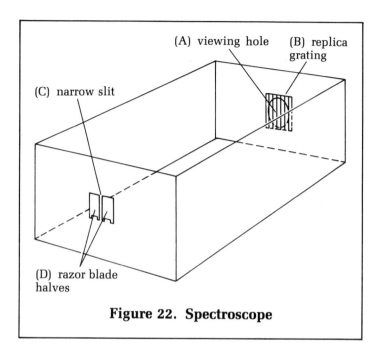

(A) viewing hole   (B) replica grating

(C) narrow slit

(D) razor blade halves

Figure 22. Spectroscope

Examining the Spectrum of a Fluorescent Lamp

Use your spectroscope to examine the spectrum produced by a fluorescent lamp. The slit in the spectroscope must be parallel to the axis of the lamp. Describe the spectrum that you observe. Make a colored diagram of the spectrum.

Additional Projects

1. Compare the light spectra produced by various types of "neon" lamps. Some "neon" lamps actually contain the element neon, while others contain different gases, such as argon or krypton. Examine "neon" lights of as many different colors

as possible. Make colored diagrams that show how the spectra you observe differ from each other.

2. Study the spectra produced by sunlight *reflected* off a flat sheet of white paper and by light from an incandescent white light bulb. Find out how the white light from these two sources is the same and how it is different. *Caution:* **Never look directly at the sun. You can cause permanent damage to your eyes if you do.**

One way to view sunlight is to point the spectroscope to the right or left of the sun *but not directly at it.* Or you can look at sunlight reflected from a shiny surface. *Before working on this project, have your adult partner approve any method you devise.*

3. Invent a method for photographing the spectra produced by your spectroscope. Think about ways of using a pinhole camera (see earlier project) to make the photograph.

4. Devise a technique for studying the spectra produced by any one or more solid elements. The elements must be heated to a high temperature to yield a spectrum. Some elements to consider include iron, tin, and aluminum.

5. You can also observe the spectra of elements from compounds in which they occur. For example, by heating sodium chloride (table salt), you can observe the spectrum of sodium. Try throwing a few grains of salt on a lit stove burner. A common laboratory procedure for observing spectra is to dip a platinum wire into a sample of the salt and then to heat the wire in a very hot flame. As the salt vaporizes, it will produce a characteristic spectrum. Before working on this project, have

your adult partner approve any method you devise.

CLOUD CHAMBER

The radiation given off by radioactive materials cannot be detected directly by any of the five human senses. If you were standing next to a radioactive material, you could not see, hear, smell, taste, or feel the radiation being given off by that object. Scientists have invented devices to detect such radiation. The cloud chamber described in this section is one such device. One way detection devices are used is to find out if a person, an object, or a room has been contaminated with a radioactive material.

Detection devices are also used in scientific research. For example, they help scientists understand what happens inside particle accelerators— atom smashers. Detection devices make use of the fact that most forms of radiation cause atoms to break apart into two separate, charged parts, called ions. That process is called ionization. Devices then detect these charged particles in some way. In a cloud chamber, the charged particles cause a vapor to condense into tiny droplets. What you see in a cloud chamber is a tiny track of droplets that condense along the path taken by radiation as it passes through the chamber.

Another detection device, shown in Photo 18, is the bubble chamber. Your homemade cloud chamber probably won't resemble this complex device, but it can do some of the same things. Do some reading to find out how a bubble chamber works. (Check encyclopedias or science books, for example, the author's book *Particle Accelerators*, listed in the Bibliography.)

[119]

Photo 18. A bubble chamber, an
instrument for detecting atomic particles

Safety Note: Rubbing alcohol is poisonous and flammable. Be careful that you do not put any into your mouth. If you somehow do, notify an adult immediately. Keep the alcohol away from sparks, open flames, or excessive heat. Dry ice can damage skin. Wear gloves and protective clothing when you handle it. Use tongs to pick it up.

Materials: scissors; black blotting paper or black felt; ruler; pencil; large jar with cover that fits tightly, such as a large peanut butter jar; glue; dry ice slightly larger in size than the diameter of the jar; old bathroom or kitchen towel; rubbing alcohol; source of bright light, such as the lamp in a slide projector; radioactive material (see caution below). *Note:* If you cannot find dry ice, you can collect solid carbon dioxide by spraying the gas from a fire extinguisher onto a sheet of Styrofoam. Attempt this procedure only if your adult partner is present to observe your work.

Directions

Note: Letters in parentheses—for example, (A)—are keyed in to Figure 23.

1.   Cut a piece of the blotting paper or felt to fit the bottom of the jar. Glue the paper or felt (A) to the bottom of the jar.

2.   Cut a second strip of the blotting paper or felt about 2 inches wide and long enough to fit around the inside of the jar. Glue the strip (B) around the inside of the jar, at the bottom, next to the paper or felt on the jar bottom.

3.   Cut a piece of the blotting paper or felt (C) to fit the inside of the jar cap. Glue the material to the inside of the jar cap.

[121]

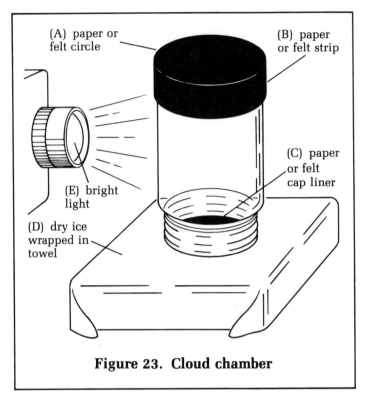

(A) paper or felt circle

(B) paper or felt strip

(C) paper or felt cap liner

(E) bright light

(D) dry ice wrapped in towel

Figure 23. Cloud chamber

4.   Allow the glue to dry thoroughly before proceeding. The cloud chamber will not perform correctly unless the glue is completely dry.

5.   Use tongs to wrap the dry ice in the towel and place it (D) on a tabletop.

6.   Warm the jar by running it under hot water for a couple of minutes.

7.   Saturate the blotting paper or felt on the bottom of the jar (but not the cap) with rubbing alcohol.

8.   Quickly screw the cap on the jar, invert the jar, and place it upside down on the dry ice.

9.   Shine the bright light (E) through the middle of the jar. The light must be intense (at least 200 watts), with as narrow a beam as possible.

Radiation from a Radioactive Material

Caution: Work under supervision of a qualified science teacher, scientist, or medical professional. Always wear goggles, gloves, and protective clothing when you work with radioactive materials. Use tongs or forceps to handle the materials. Use only those materials approved by your supervisor.

Obtain a piece of radioactive material that you may safely use from your supervisor. Or you can use the mantle from a portable gas lantern (*still working under supervision*). The mantle contains a small amount of the radioactive element thorium. Place the mantle or the material next to the cloud chamber. Look for tracks inside the jar caused by radiation from the material. Make a sketch of any tracks that you see.

Additional Projects

1.   How do your results differ if the radioactive source is placed *outside* the cloud chamber? Try placing the source next to the chamber, at a distance of 1 inch, 2 inches, 3 inches, and so on. Can you observe any differences in the tracks you observe in each of these cases?

2.   Radiation is always present in the natural environment. Place the cloud chamber in a place where no known radioactive material is present. Watch for tracks in the cloud chamber from this "background radiation."

3.   Devise a method for counting the amount of background radiation detected by your cloud chamber.

4.   Ask your supervisor for a selection of radioactive isotopes. Find out how the tracks in the cloud chamber differ, if at all, for the various materials.

5.   Radiation can be stopped by using the proper amount of "shielding" material, such as paper, cloth, wood, and different metals. Use the cloud chamber to find out the thickness of various shielding materials needed to stop the radiation from one of the radioactive sources provided by your supervisor.

6.   Bring in samples of rocks that you find in your neighborhood. Find out if any one kind of rock seems to contain radioactive materials. If so, are radioactive materials more abundant in some types of rocks than in others?

SOLAR HEATER

Solar energy—energy from the sun—is a readily available, relatively inexpensive source of power, although humans have yet to develop devices that make full use of this important energy source. The solar heater is an example of the kind of device that can capture, concentrate, and make use of solar energy.

The shape of the solar heater described below is critical. The figure you reproduce is a parabola, a geometric figure that has a useful property in this device. Every light ray that strikes the parabola will reflect to the same point in the middle of the figure. Thus, the sunlight that strikes all parts of the parabola are brought to focus along the axis of the solar heater.

Safety Note: Be sure to work under supervision and wear safety goggles. Make sure that you know how to use a jigsaw safely and properly. Ask your adult partner to demonstrate its use and to supervise your use of the saw.

Materials: pencil; sheet of white cardboard, about 2 inches × 10 inches × 8 inches; scissors; two pieces of wood, 1 inch × 8 inches × 4 inches; jigsaw; three 1-inch wooden dowels, 10 inches long; glue or hammer and nails; two wooden boards, 1 inch × 8 inches × 8 inches; wooden board, 2 inches × 8 inches × 12 inches; drill or brace and bit; steel wire, at least 20 inches long; stapler; steel wool; heavy-duty aluminum foil (one roll); tacks; two bolts and wing nuts; large metal cap or plastic cup; watch or clock.

Directions

Note: Letters in parentheses—for example, (A)—are keyed in to Figure 24.

1.   With the pencil, copy the parabolic curve (A) *exactly* onto the white cardboard.

2.   With the scissors, cut out the parabola and use it as a pattern to draw the some curve on each of the 1 inch × 8 inch × 4 inch boards. With the jigsaw (*careful!*), cut both parabolas out of the wooden boards.

3.   Join the two wooden parabolas (B) with the three dowels (C) by gluing or nailing them as shown.

[125]

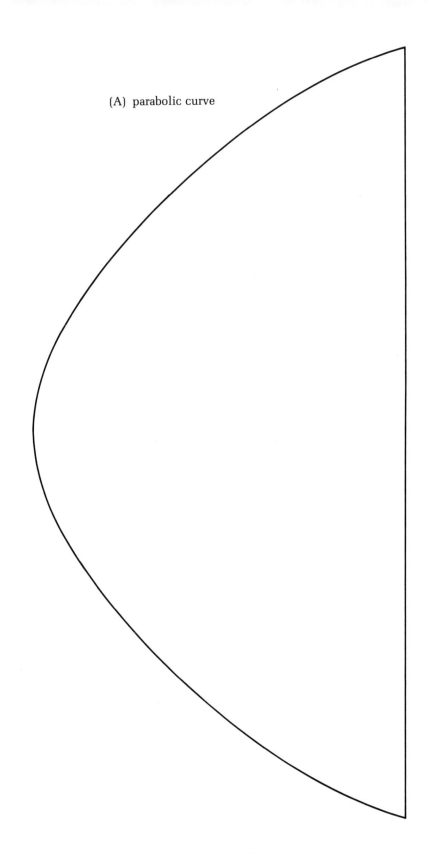

(A) parabolic curve

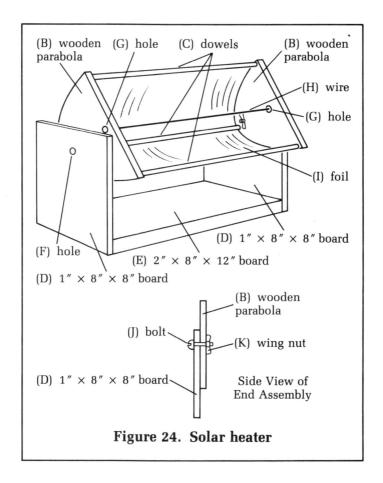

(B) wooden parabola (G) hole (C) dowels (B) wooden parabola

(H) wire

(G) hole

(I) foil

(D) 1″ × 8″ × 8″ board

(F) hole

(E) 2″ × 8″ × 12″ board

(D) 1″ × 8″ × 8″ board

(B) wooden parabola

(J) bolt

(K) wing nut

(D) 1″ × 8″ × 8″ board

Side View of End Assembly

Figure 24. Solar heater

4.   Make the support stand by gluing or nailing the 1 inch × 8 inch × 8 inch boards (D) to the 2 inch × 8 inch × 12 inch board (E). With the drill or brace and bit, drill a hole (F) in the middle of each vertical board about 1 inch from the top.

5.   Drill a hole (G) near the center of the flat edge of each wooden parabola. Run the steel wire (H) from the hole in one wooden parabola to the hole in the other wooden parabola. Pull the wire tight

and staple it at one end. Loop the other end through the hole a couple of times. The wire is used to hang things on.

6. With the steel wool, clean the aluminum foil well. Attach the aluminum foil (I) to the wooden parabolic supports, shiny side inward, with tacks. Pull the foil as tightly as possible to the supports (but don't tear it!) and keep it as smooth as you can. If the foil gets wrinkled, the solar heater will not work efficiently.

7. Attach the parabolic aluminum–wood frame to the vertical wooden supports using bolts (J) and wing nuts (K) at each end. The aluminum–wood frame should be held in place snugly, but you should be able to rotate the frame as necessary.

Heating Water

Caution: **Do not look directly into the parabolic mirror assembly when it is pointed at the sun. Severe eye damage, possibly resulting in blindness, may occur.**

Make a bucket of the large metal cap or plastic cup. Punch two holes opposite each other near the rim of the cap or cup and thread the wire in the middle of the solar heater through both holes. To thread the bucket, first unwrap the end of the wire that is not stapled to an end piece. Run the loose end of the wire through the two holes in the bucket and then through the hole in the end piece. Loop the wire through the hole, as before. The bucket must hang as close to the center of the heater as possible. Half-fill the bucket with water. Rotate the heater until it points directly at the sun. Note the temperature of the water at 5-minute intervals for about a half hour. Make a graph of your observations.

Additional Projects

1.   Find a way to use your solar heater to cook a hot dog.

2.   Find out how the amount an object is heated is affected by the distance that object is placed away from the central wire.

3.   Devise a method for focusing the heater at the best possible position with respect to the sun.

4.   Invent a method for placing an object to be heated precisely on the axis of the heater.

5.   Consult a physics or physical science laboratory manual to find experiments that require the heating of a material. For example, some manuals describe experiments designed to test the effect of color on the amount of heat absorbed by an object. Others show how to determine the relative ability of different metals to conduct heat (their "conductivity"). Adapt one or more of those experiments in order that they can be used with your solar heater.

CALORIMETER

A calorimeter measures the energy content of some substances. A common use of a calorimeter is determining the energy content of foods. In this application, a food is burned and the heat produced is used to warm water. By measuring the increase in temperature of the water, you can calculate the amount of energy released, in Calories, during the burning of the food. The efficiency of a calorimeter depends very much on the extent to which the heat released during burning goes to heating the water and is not lost to the environment surrounding the calorimeter.

Materials: hammer and nail; cat food or tuna fish can; large straight pin or needle; soldering iron; glue; wooden board, 2 inches × 6 inches × 6 inches; no. 10 tin can; tin snips; heavy wire gauze (window screen can be used if it is made of very heavy screening); sharp knife; Styrofoam box, large enough to hold calorimeter; peanut; balance; Celsius thermometer.

Directions

Note: Letters in parentheses—for example, (A)—are keyed in to Figure 25.

1.   With the hammer and nail, make a small hole in the bottom of the cat food or tuna fish can (A). Insert the straight pin or needle into the hole, sharp side up. With the soldering iron, solder the pin or needle (B) to the can.

2.   Glue the can to the wooden board (C).

3.   With the tin snips, cut out one section of the no. 10 tin can to form a stand as shown in the diagram (D). *Caution:* **Be very careful in cutting the tin can, as the edges will be very sharp.** Ask your adult partner to observe you when you cut the can.

4.   Use the tin snips to cut the wire gauze (E) in a circle just slightly larger than the diameter of the tin can. Make sure the gauze is heavy enough to support the glass jar that will be placed on it.

5.   Place the board and cat food or tuna fish can inside the tin can stand.

6.   With the sharp knife, carefully remove one side of the Styrofoam box (F) and slide the tin can stand, wooden board, and can into the box.

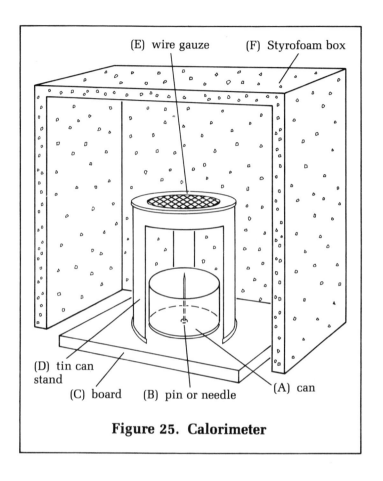

(E) wire gauze   (F) Styrofoam box

(D) tin can
stand
(C) board   (B) pin or needle   (A) can

Figure 25. Calorimeter

Finding the Energy Content of a Peanut

Safety Note: Do this project only in the presence of your adult partner.

Weigh a single peanut as exactly as you can. Since *Calories* are a unit in the metric system, you will have to use that system in this project. Stick the peanut on the pin or needle. Place a heatproof glass container on a wire gauze on top of the tin can stand. Add about 100 milliliters of water to the container. Read and record the temperature of the

[131]

water in degrees Celsius. Set fire to the peanut. Note and record the highest temperature reached by the water. *Caution:* **Be careful not to ignite the Styrofoam.**

You can calculate the energy content of the peanut by using the following formula:

$$\text{Number of Calories (per gram of food)} = \frac{\text{weight of water (in grams)} \times \text{increase in temperature (in } ^\circ \text{C)}}{\text{weight of food (in grams)} \times 1000}$$

Additional Projects

1. Repeat the above project using larger and smaller amounts of water. See what effect these changes have on your results.

2. Determine the heat content of other kinds of nuts by the method described above.

3. Devise a method for calculating the energy content of other types of foods, such as a piece of bread or dried fruit.

4. The calorimeter can also be used to determine the heat content of various fuels. Measure the heat content of paper, wood, charcoal, and any other solid material that you think might be used as a fuel. *Caution:* **Do not use any liquid fuels and be sure you get the approval of your adult partner before testing *any* material.**

5. Can the spring balance used in Chapter One be used to measure mass in this project? Design a project that will show how accurate the spring balance is for this purpose.

CHROMATOGRAPHIC COLUMN

Scientists often want to separate the components of a mixture from one another. One method for making separations like this is called chromatography. For example, food chemists use chromatography to separate and identify the substances responsible for the flavor and odor of foods.

Many types of chromatography are now in use. They all depend on the fact that various components of a mixture flow through a fluid (a gas or a liquid) at different rates. The liquid column device described here allows you not only to separate a mixture into its components, but also to capture each component for further study. For example, you can use this method to identify the materials that make up the green coloring in leaves.

Safety Note: Review the cautions in Appendix 1 about working with glass. Work under supervision and wear safety goggles and a lab coat or apron. Use caution in working with flames.

Materials: triangular file; pencil and ruler; glass tube, about 12 inches long and no less than ½ inch in inner diameter; Bunsen or alcohol burner; glass wool; glass tube, about 2 inches long, to fit rubber stopper; one-hole rubber stopper to fit 12-inch glass tube; rubber tubing, about 2 inches long, to fit short glass tube; screw clamp; ring stand; ring clamp or burette clamp; silica gel, 28-200 mesh (ask a chemistry teacher for this material); beaker or jar; colored liquid mixture, such as colored ink, vegetable dye, or food coloring; eyedropper.

Directions

Note: Letters in parentheses—for example, (A)—are keyed in to Figure 26.

1.   Read the instructions in Appendix 1 about cutting and fire-polishing glass tubing. Cut and fire-polish the longer piece of glass tubing (A). Select a size of tubing that will take the smallest rubber stopper you can find. A no. 00 rubber stopper is the smallest stopper commercially available.

2.   Insert a small wad of the glass wool (B) about ½ inch into the end of the tube.

3.   Cut and fire-polish the shorter piece of glass tubing.

4.   Insert the short glass tube (C) into the one-hole rubber stopper (D) so that it is flush with the narrow end of the stopper.

5.   Insert the rubber stopper into the longer glass tube so that it is in contact with the glass wool.

6.   Attach the rubber tubing (E) to the glass tube in the rubber stopper and attach the screw clamp (F) to the rubber tubing.

7.   Support the glass tube on the ring stand (G) with the ring clamp or burette clamp (H).

8.   Make a slurry by adding water to 28-200 mesh silica gel in the beaker or jar. The slurry should have the consistency of thin oatmeal.

9.   Pour the slurry into the top of the glass tube. Fill the tube about two-thirds of the way up with the silica gel (I). The water from the slurry will begin to drain through the glass tube in the bottom of the column, while the silica gel remains in the tube.

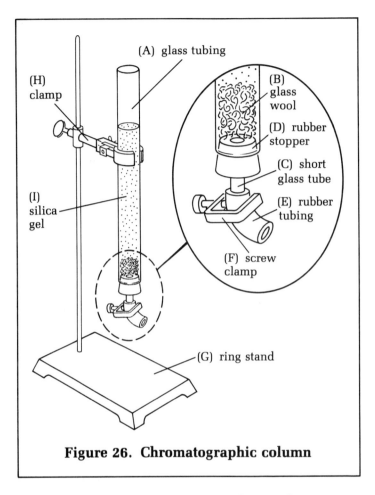

(A) glass tubing

(H) clamp

(B) glass wool

(D) rubber stopper

(C) short glass tube

(I) silica gel

(E) rubber tubing

(F) screw clamp

(G) ring stand

Figure 26. Chromatographic column

Separating a Mixture of Liquids

Now you can use your chromatography tube for an experiment. Select a colored liquid mixture that you would like to separate into its component parts. Colored ink, a vegetable dye, and food coloring are possible samples.

When one of these liquid mixtures is poured through the tube, each component of the mixture moves through the silica gel at a different speed.

[135]

Those that move rapidly will tend to concentrate near the bottom of the tube. Those that move slowly will concentrate near the top. A short while after pouring the liquid mixture through the tube, you should see a series of rings forming in the tube. Each ring corresponds to one component (or a group of closely related components) of the mixture.

To begin your separation, add water to the top of the column until about an inch remains above the gel. Then use the eyedropper to add about 10 drops of the liquid mixture to be separated to the top of the column. Finally, add additional water to the column until you see the liquid mixture moving down the column.

You can control the rate at which the liquid mixture moves through the column by tightening or loosening the screw clamp.

Eventually you should be able to observe a number of rings forming in the column. Each ring corresponds to at least one component of the ink or dye mixture you are analyzing.

Additional Projects

1. Repeat the introductory experiment with other liquid mixtures that consist of two or more liquids.

2. A plant leaf contains a number of colored components. Separate those components by means of chromatography. First, with a pestle, grind up the plant leaf in a mortar. Add a little white sand to the mortar as you grind up the leaf. Then dissolve the colored components in denatured alcohol. You can substitute rubbing (isopropyl) alcohol for the denatured alcohol. Pour the col-

ored alcohol solution through the chromatography column. In this case, alcohol, rather than water, is used as the solvent in separating the components of the mixture. *Caution:* **Denatured alcohol and rubbing alcohol are both toxic and flammable.** Do not put either liquid into your mouth. If you do so by accident, immediately notify an adult. Keep all alcohols away from sparks and open flames. Have a fire extinguisher at hand.

3. Repeat Project 2 using a flower instead of a leaf.

4. The rings formed in a chromatography column are sometimes fuzzy. This may mean that the ring contains more than one component. A particular type of ink could, for example, contain two components, both of which move down the column at almost the same rate. Invent a method for separating the components of a fuzzy ring.

5. Find a way to remove each component of a liquid mixture from a chromatography column, one at a time.

6. Determine the effect of using solids other than silica gel and liquid other than water in the chromatography tube. Obtain an adult's approval before using any material other than silica gel and water.

APPENDIX 1

WORKING WITH

GLASS

Working with glass is an old art, and techniques such as glassblowing are thousands of years old. Building and using some of the equipment in this book doesn't require anything as sophisticated as glassblowing, but it does require a knowledge of several techniques, along with the safety procedures involved.

Glass tubing is used in many types of scientific equipment. It comes in many different sizes. The size of glass tubing is usually indicated by its outer diameter (o.d.), although its inner diameter (i.d.) may also be specified. Unless otherwise specified, the size of glass tubing to use for instruments described in this book is that with an outer diameter of about 8 millimeters.

The main techniques referred to in this book are (1) cutting glass tubing, (2) fire-polishing the ends, (3) bending the tubing, and (4) inserting glass tubing into rubber stoppers.

[139]

Caution: **Glass can shatter and cut you or fly into your face and eyes; sharp edges can cut you. Hot glass can burn you, and the flame from a Bunsen or alcohol burner also can burn you. If not made and used properly, glass tubing can cause serious injuries.**

To minimize hazards and ensure successful results,

- Always work under direct supervision of a qualified science teacher or scientist.
- Wear safety goggles, protective gloves, and a lab apron when cutting, fire-polishing, or bending glass tubing.
- Keep your lab space neat and clean.
- Keep safety, fire-extinguishing, and first-aid equipment where you work.

GLASS CUTTING

Glass tubing is cut with a triangular file. Lay the tubing on a tabletop and draw the file firmly across it, away from your body. If the file is sharp, you can make a sharp, deep scratch with only two or three strokes. If the file is not sharp, you may have to draw the file across the glass a few more times. In no case should you ever "saw" on the glass, as it may splinter and cut you. See Photo 19.

When it is apparent that you have made a definite groove in the tubing, pick up the glass in both hands and wrap a towel around it. Turn the grooved side of the glass away from you and place both thumbs next to the scratch you have made. Then, gently draw the ends of the tubing toward you. See Photo 20.

If the scratch is deep enough, the tubing will

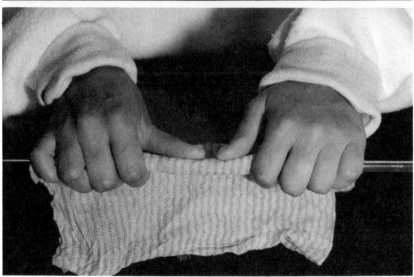

PHOTOS 19 AND 20. When cutting glass tubing, the first step is to use a file to make a scratch on the tube. The second step in cutting glass tubing is to break the glass as shown.

snap easily, leaving a clean, sharp edge on both pieces. Do not try to force the tube toward you, as it may shatter. Should the tubing not break easily, try scratching it a little more deeply with a few more strokes of the file. When the tubing has been scratched deeply enough, it will break with little effort.

FIRE-POLISHING

The edges on a freshly cut piece of glass are very sharp. If left that way, such glass would be dangerous to work with. The next step, therefore, is to fire-polish the ends of the glass tubing. During fire-polishing, the glass begins to melt and, in so doing, rounds off.

Lay the glass tubing across the open fingers of the left hand. Hold the tubing so that the end is over the flame of a Bunsen or alcohol burner. Rotate the tubing slowly with your right hand. Make sure that all sides of the tubing get heated equally. The glass will get yellow, and the cut edge will start to look smooth. Don't heat the ends too long as they will eventually begin to seal up. See Photo 21.

Caution: **Hot glass looks just like cool glass. Be careful when you pick up a piece of glass tubing that you have been working with to make sure that it is not hot.**

GLASS BENDING

Making scientific equipment often requires that you bend a piece of glass tubing into some particular shape. The technique is easy to learn, and once you have mastered the skill, you can make

PHOTO 21. Fire-polishing the
end of a length of glass tubing

almost any shape you want with a piece of glass-tubing.

An important secret in glass bending is to heat as wide an area as possible on the glass in the region where you want to make your bend. School laboratories have *wing tops* or *fishtails* to spread out the flame of a burner. If you do not have access to such equipment, you can achieve a similar result simply by moving the glass tubing back and forth, heating a wide area on it equally.

To begin with, try making a right-angle bend in a glass tube.

As you did in fire-polishing, lay the glass tubing across the open fingers of your left hand. Hold the tubing so that the area to be bent is over the flame of a Bunsen or alcohol burner. (See photo.) Rotate the tubing slowly with your right hand.

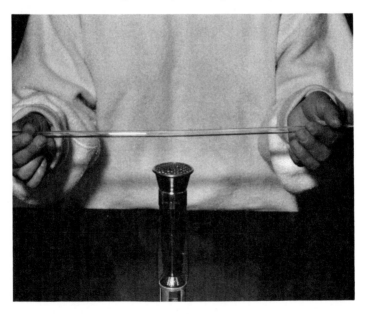

Photo 22. *Bending a piece of glass tubing*

Make sure that all sides of the tube are heated equally. When the tube gets hot enough, remove it from the flame and slowly pull both ends toward you until the tube forms a right-angle bend.

This direction sounds simple enough, but it can be quite difficult. The problem lies in knowing exactly when the tube is ready to bend. If you try bending before it is hot enough, the glass may break. If you wait too long, the glass may melt and begin to sag.

Experience is the best way to know when to make your bend. One clue is that the glass will begin to glow with an orange color as it begins to get hot. You will probably feel the glass beginning to get soft at this point. Now is the time to make the bend. If you've guessed wrong about the timing, the glass will either shatter or form a strange-looking angle. Don't worry. Get another piece of glass and try again. Before long, you will develop the sense of touch that lets you know when the bend should be made.

INSERTING GLASS TUBES

Many times it is necessary to insert a glass tube into a rubber stopper. This procedure can be difficult because the glass tube usually has the same diameter as that of the hole in the stopper. *Caution:* **If you try to force the tubing into the stopper, the glass is likely to shatter and cause serious injury to your hands**.

Here are the proper steps for inserting a glass tube into a rubber stopper:

1. Start by lubricating the inside of the hole in the stopper and the outside of the glass tubing. Use

a little water or a drop of oil, glycerine, or petroleum jelly.

2. Hold the glass tube and the rubber stopper with a cloth towel. Wrap the towel around the glass tube near the end to be inserted into the stopper. DO NOT let the end of the tubing press against the palm of your hand.

3. Push the tube into the hole gently, using a twisting movement. DO NOT try to force the tube directly into the hole. With patience, a back-and-forth twisting motion will gradually work the glass tube into the rubber stopper. See Photo 23.

With patience and practice, you should have no trouble becoming proficient in the art of working with glass.

PHOTO 23. Inserting a glass tube into a rubber stopper

APPENDIX 2

SCIENTIFIC SUPPLY COMPANIES

Please note that some scientific supply companies will sell directly to individuals but others will not. Call or write the company directly for further information.

Carolina Biological Supply
2700 York Road
Burlington, NC 27215
(919) 584-0381

Central Scientific Company (CENCO)
11222 Melrose Avenue
Franklin Park, IL 60131
(312) 451-0150 or
(800) 262-3626

Connecticut Valley Biological Supply
82 Valley Road, P. O. Box 326
Southampton, MA 01073
(800) 628-7748 [or
(800) 282-7757 in Massachusetts]

Delta Education
P.O. Box M
Nashua, NH 03061-6012
(603) 889-8899 or (800) 258-1302

Edmund Scientific
101 E. Gloucester Pike
Barrington, NJ 08007
(609) 573-6250 or (609) 573-6925

Fisher Scientific
4901 W. LeMoyne Street
Chicago, IL 60651
(312) 378-7770 or (800) 621-4769

Frey Scientific
905 Hickory Lane
Mansfield, OH 44905
(419) 589-9905

McKilligan Supply
435 Main Street
Johnson City, NY 13790
(607) 729-6511

Nasco
901 Janesville Avenue
Fort Atkinson, WI 53538
(414) 563-2446 or (800) 558-9595

Nasco West
P.O. Box 3837
Modesto, CA 95352
(209) 529-6957

Northwest Scientific
4311 Anthony Court, #700, P.O. Box 305
Rocklin, CA 95677
(916) 652-9229 or FAX (916) 652-9674

Powell Laboratories
Box 187
Gladstone, OR 97027
(503) 656-1641

Sargent-Welch Scientific
7350 N. Linder Avenue
Skokie, IL 60077
(800) SARGENT

Schoolmasters Science
745 State Circle, P.O. Box 1941
Ann Arbor, MI 48106
(313) 761-5072

Scientific Kit and Boreal Lab
777 E. Park Drive
Tonawanda, NY 14150
(716) 874-6020 or
FAX (716) 874-9572

BIBLIOGRAPHY

Arnov, Boris. *Water: Experiments to Understand It.* New York: Lothrop, Lee, & Shepard, 1980.

Bachert, Russell E., Jr., and Emerson L. Snooks. *Outdoor Education Equipment.* Danville, Ill.: The Interstate Printers, 1974.

Barrett, Raymond, E. *Build-It-Yourself Science Laboratory.* Garden City, N.Y.: Doubleday, 1963.

Bartholomew, Roland B., and Frank E. Crawley. *Science Laboratory Techniques.* Menlo Park, Calif.: Addison-Wesley, 1980.

Bender, Alfred. *The Electron.* New York: Sentinel Books, 1960.

Bleifeld, Maurice. *Experimenting with a Microscope.* New York: Franklin Watts, 1988.

Cobb, Vicki. *Chemically Active!* New York: Lippincott, 1985.

Gardner, Robert. *Famous Experiments You Can Do.* New York: Franklin Watts, 1990.

———. *Ideas for Science Projects.* New York:

Franklin Watts, 1986. Contains projects in all the sciences.

———. *More Ideas for Science Projects.* New York: Franklin Watts, 1989. Contains projects in all the sciences.

Guidebook to Constructing Inexpensive Science Teaching Equipment, Vol. I: Biology; Vol. II: Chemistry; Vol. III: Physics. College Park, Md.: Science Teaching Center, University of Maryland, 1972.

Lowery, Lawrence F. *The Everyday Science Sourcebook.* Palo Alto, Calif.: Dale Seymour, 1985.

Markle, Sandra. *Weather, Electricity, Environmental Investigations.* Santa Barbara, Calif: Learning Works, 1982.

Newton, David E. *Consumer Chemistry Projects for Young Scientists.* New York: Franklin Watts, 1990.

———. *Particle Accelerators: From the Cyclotron to the Superconducting Super Collider.* New York: Franklin Watts, 1989.

———. *Science/Technology/Society Projects for Young Scientists.* New York: Franklin Watts, 1991. Includes many environmental projects.

New UNESCO Source Book for Science Teaching. Paris: UNESCO, 1973.

Oleksy, Walter. *Experiments with Heat.* Chicago: Childrens Press, 1986.

Prochnow, Dave. *101 Experiments for the Young Scientist.* Blue Ridge Summit, Pa.: TAB Books, 1988.

Renner, Al G. *How to Make and Use a Microlab.* New York: Putnam, 1971.

Roberts, Hortense Roberta. *You Can Make an Insect Zoo*. Chicago: Childrens Press, 1974.

Science Works: An Ontario Science Centre Book of Experiments. Toronto: Kids Can Press, 1984.

Simon, Seymour. *Science Projects in Ecology*. New York: Holiday House, 1972. Includes projects with insects, among other topics.

————. *Science Projects in Pollution*. New York: Holiday House, 1972.

Sootin, Harry. *Easy Experiments with Water Pollution*. New York: Four Winds Press, 1974.

Stanley, Leon R. *Easy to Make Electric Gadgets*. New York: Harvey House, 1980.

Tannenbaum, Beulah, and Harold E. Tannenbaum. *Making and Using Your Own Weather Station*. New York: Franklin Watts, 1989.

Tocci, Salvatore. *Chemistry Around You*. New York: Prentice-Hall, 1985.

Trowbridge, Leslie W. *Experiments in Meteorology*. Garden City, N.Y.: Doubleday, 1973.

Van Cleave, Janice. *Physics for Every Kid*. New York: John Wiley, 1991.

INDEX

Page numbers in *italics* refer to illustrations.